Treaties and Indigenous Peoples

TREATIES AND INDIGENOUS PEOPLES

THE ROBB LECTURES 1991

IAN BROWNLIE, Q.C.

Edited by F. M. BROOKFIELD

CLARENDON PRESS · OXFORD

1992

This book has been printed digitally and produced in a standard design in order to ensure its continuing availability

OXFORD
UNIVERSITY PRESS

Great Clarendon Street, Oxford OX2 6DP

Oxford University Press is a department of the University of Oxford. It furthers the University's objective of excellence in research, scholarship, and education by publishing worldwide in

Oxford New York

Athens Auckland Bangkok Bogotá Buenos Aires Cape Town Chennai Dar es Salaam Delhi Florence Hong Kong Istanbul Karachi Kolkata Kuala Lumpur Madrid Melbourne Mexico City Mumbai Nairobi Paris São Paulo Shanghai Singapore Taipei Tokyo Toronto Warsaw

with associated companies in Berlin Ibadan

Oxford is a registered trade mark of Oxford University Press in the UK and in certain other countries

Published in the United States by Oxford University Press Inc., New York

Reprinted 2001

ISBN 0-19-825716-3

THE ROBB LECTURES

The Robb Lectures are given annually in the University of Auckland, by internationally distinguished scholars, in commemoration of the late Sir Douglas Robb, Chancellor of the University from 1962 to 1968 and pre-eminent in the establishing of its School of Medicine.

Foreword

The four lectures of which this little book consists were delivered at the University of Auckland in an annual series in commemoration of the late Sir Douglas Robb, Chancellor of the University from 1962 to 1968.

The theme is the Treaty of Waitangi, concluded in 1840, and the recent enhancement of the legal status of the Treaty within New Zealand. However, the essential purpose of the lectures is to examine the difficult question of group rights within the specific context of the Maori claims to the recreation of equitable relations between Maori and Pakeha. Thus the concepts of self-determination, of minority rights, and of indigenous peoples, are examined in the light of international law and the standards of human rights.

Whilst the situation of the Maori in New Zealand has special features, among which the Treaty of Waitangi is pre-eminent, it is necessary to refer to the framework of human rights and of standard-setting multilateral treaties to which New Zealand is a Party. This broad framework, and the growing importance of group rights on every side, ensure that the subject-matter has a general relevance. In the result there is a useful traffic between the general and the particular.

The author of the lectures is a public international lawyer who has experience in human rights matters as a professional lawyer. The approach has been to attempt to produce an analytical schema of the problems of the kind necessary in providing objective advice to a client. The primary pursuit has not been an obvious virtue but a greater understanding, and those who prefer simple choices may find it necessary to adjust their parameters.

The text now offered is identical with the lectures as they were delivered, but with certain limited corrections and emendations. In particular, the New Zealand material has been carefully checked by Professor Brookfield and where necessary certain corrections have been made. In the course of editing the text, Professor Brookfield has considerably enhanced and updated the references. The legal position is stated as at the beginning of September 1991.

IAN BROWNLIE
F. M. BROOKFIELD

Preface and Acknowledgements

AT the outset I wish to thank the University of Auckland and the Trustees of the fund created to commemorate the late Sir Douglas Robb for the invitation to give these lectures, and I must explain why I accepted the invitation. The attraction was not the opportunity to travel, since I travel frequently on professional business; rather it was the nature of the subject and the fact that it presents substantial difficulties.

That is not sufficient excuse, however. There is already a rich outpouring of good-quality writing about the Treaty of Waitangi and the relations of Maori and Pakeha.* What, if anything, can a lawyer from elsewhere add to the existing debate? The answer, if there is one, is that the professional lawyer working in the field of international law can sometimes provide an external perspective to which the internal debate can be related. My experience is that of a practising international lawyer working normally for States but also for

* For some recent writing, see C. Orange, *The Treaty of Waitangi* (Wellington, 1987); essays by the several writers in I. H. [Sir Hugh] Kawharu (ed.), *Waitangi: Māori and Pākehā Perspectives of the Treaty of Waitangi* (Auckland, 1989); R. J. Mulgan, *Maori, Pakeha and Democracy* (Auckland, 1989); A. Sharp, *Justice and the Māori* (Auckland, 1990; repr. with corrs., 1991); articles by several writers in (1990) 14 *NZULR*, no. 1 (special Waitangi number); P. G. McHugh, 'The Role of Law in Maori Claims' (1990) *NZLJ* 16; R. P. Boast, 'Treaty Rights or Aboriginal Rights?' [1990] *NZLJ* 32; M. P. K. Sorrenson, 'Giving Better Effect to the Treaty: Some Thoughts for 1990' (1990) 24 *NZJ.Hist.* 135; F. M. Brookfield, 'Maori Rights and Two Radical Writers: Review and Response' [1990] *NZLJ* 406. See also Ch. 1, n. 6, and, for some committedly radical views, Ch. 3, n. 20. And see now, most recently published, P. [G.] McHugh, *The Māori Magna Carta: New Zealand Law and the Treaty of Waitangi* (Auckland, 1991).

national groups seeking advice on human rights and related questions. I am not an expert on the affairs of New Zealand, but I can claim experience in working outside my own community and in the application of recently developed standards of human rights in practical contexts.

I.B.

Contents

Abbreviations

Ab.LB	*Aboriginal Law Bulletin*
AC	Appeal Cases
ALR	Australian Law Reports
BYIL	*British Yearbook of International Law*
CA	Court of Appeal
Ch.	Chancery
CLR	Commonwealth Law Reports
CO 209/4	Colonial Office correspondence between the Secretary of State and the Governor of New Zealand from 1839, in the Public Record Office, London
CRNZ	Criminal Reports of New Zealand
DLR	Dominion Law Reports
GAOR	General Assembly Official Records
ILO	International Labour Organization
ILR	International Law Reports, ed. E. Lauterpacht
MLR	*Modern Law Review*
NZ Jo. Hist.	*New Zealand Journal of History*
NZ Jur. (NS)	New Zealand Jurist (New Series)
NZLJ	*New Zealand Law Journal*
NZLR	New Zealand Law Reports
NZRL	*New Zealand Recent Law*
NZRL Rev.	*New Zealand Recent Law Review*
NZULR	*New Zealand Universities Law Review*
OJLS	*Oxford Journal of Legal Studies*
OL Rev.	*Otago Law Review*
QB	Queen's Bench
SC	Supreme Court
SCC	Supreme Court of Canada

SCR	Supreme Court Reports (Canada)
UNGA	United Nations General Assembly
UNTS	*United Nations Treaty Series*
VUWLR	*Victoria University of Wellington Law Review*
WLR	Weekly Law Reports

1

Equity Between Early and Subsequent Arrivals

THE subject of these lectures is essentially the question of equity, justice, or fair dealing, between two groups which can be differentiated on the basis that one group consists of early arrivals and the other of subsequent arrivals.[1] The question may be asked, how can this be a subject worth special examination?

If a State is democratic in practice and subject to the rule of law, then each individual within it will enjoy his or her modicum of freedom, and the recognition of the rights of the individual guarantees an absence of problems. But, in the case of New Zealand, there are three dimensions to be added. The first is the existence of a group claiming a separate identity and the recognition of this claim within the prevailing political

[1] Many scholars accept that Maori first came to (a thitherto uninhabited) New Zealand about the 8th c. AD (A few estimate earlier; others that the coming was possibly later, but not after 1100.) See K. Sinclair, *A History of New Zealand*, 4th revd. edn. (Auckland, 1991), 14; R. [J.] Walker, *Ka Whawhai Tonu Matou: Struggle Without End* (Auckland, 1990), 24. For specialist discussion see e.g. J. Davidson, *The Prehistory of New Zealand*, new edn., (Auckland, 1987), chs. 1 and 2, esp. p. 1, and in W. H. Oliver (ed.) with B. R. Williams, *The Oxford History of New Zealand* (Wellington, 1981, ch. 1, esp. p. 6; and A. Anderson in D. Green (ed.), *Towards 1990* (Wellington, 1989), 1–9 (summary, assessment, and further references). European settlement, or, rather, frequenting, of New Zealand, began in the last decade of the 18th c., after the visits of James Cook (his first being in 1769) and of other navigators. Problems of law and order resulting from increasing settlement were among the factors which led to the Treaty of Waitangi and the subsequent establishment of British sovereignty in 1840. See e.g. Sinclair, *History*, pt. I, ch. 1; J. M. R. Owens, in *Oxford History*, ch. 2; C. Orange, *The Treaty of Waitangi* (Wellington, 1987), chs. 1 and 2.

and legal system. Given the structure of New Zealand society, identification of the Maori as a group must involve the implied incorporation, so to speak, of other groups, including Pakeha and recent migrants from Pacific islands. The recognition of group identity as such would not, in normal circumstances, involve serious structural problems. It is common for group identity to depend upon the use of a language, the education of children in the language of the family, adherence to a particular religion, or adherence to particular cultural patterns. All these questions involve problems of equality and non-discrimination, but they can be, and usually are, resolved within the normal pattern of constitutional law with some prompting from the obligations arising from fairly recent multilateral agreements codifying standards of human rights.

There is a second added dimension which presents formidable problems, and that is the attachment of the Maori as a group to the rightful possession of land.[2] The issue here is not *access* to land and natural resources, although that may be a significant outcome. The issue is *entitlement* to particular land areas. Moreover, the entitlement in principle is based on 1840 as a critical date[3] and the resulting claims necessarily put in issue the legality and justice of interim transfers and leases out of Maori possession.

The third and last added dimension is the (probably) unique characteristic of the situation in New Zealand: the recognition by the political and legal system that an agenda of grievances exists, and that in the practical

[2] Maori tribes (iwi) and sub-tribes (hapu) claimed the whole of Aotearoa–New Zealand, not merely those parts in direct occupation and cultivation. See Orange, *Treaty*, 98–100; P. Adams, *Fatal Necessity: British Intervention in New Zealand 1830–1847* (Auckland, 1977), ch. 6.

[3] 1840, the year of foundation of the British colony, was decided in the (Maori) Land Court (see n. 7 below) as the year at which Maori communal entitlements to land (by possession of it in accordance with customary rules) were to be regarded as fixed. See I. H. Kawharu, *Maori Land Tenure* (Oxford, 1977), 73 (citing Judge Fenton, 1866).

sphere steps should be taken to recreate equitable relations between Maori and Pakeha.

It is these three added dimensions, taken together, and with cumulative effect, which produce the exceptional family of problems which are the real subject of debate in relation to the Treaty of Waitangi. It is intended to approach these problems from several directions. In this lecture, I shall begin to explore the role of the Treaty of Waitangi and its relationship with other means available for the recognition and enhancement of group rights will be explored. In the second lecture the broad framework, within which group rights and the principle of self-determination are recognized by international law, will be exposed. The perspective will be essentially international and the purpose will be to demonstrate the relevance or otherwise of the self-determination model to the situation in New Zealand. The third lecture will be concerned with the concept of indigenous peoples and its relevance to New Zealand, and the fourth lecture will gather the various strands together, being devoted to a final appraisal of the role of the Treaty of Waitangi.

The initial task then is to examine some of the more or less standard models of colonization and settlement. There are, of course, many variations, but five basic types will be sufficient to provide a picture.

1. Extension of power without any influx of settlers and the ultimate recovery of independence with little or no demographic change due to the period of colonial rule. Ghana and Nigeria are straightforward examples of this type.
2. The classical process of colonization with significant but localized settlement by outsiders. The British colonizations of Kenya and Southern Rhodesia fall into this category. When decolonization takes place, the settlers may be allowed to stay, but on the basis of

taking citizenship and being willing to remain as a normal component of a multiracial society. In particular, the settlers do not become a dominant element.

3. A brutal and persistent process of extermination of the original population, or expulsion from their lands, with the result that the original people literally disappear, and no potential claimants are allowed to remain. This has been the fate of the Indian population of much of southern and central Argentina.

4. Self-determination: this is also very radical, and was politically popular at the time of the Peace Settlement of 1919–20 in Europe. The application of the principle of self-determination in the European context meant that so-called minorities left on the wrong side of the boundaries of new States were given the option of changing their nationality or were sometimes the subject of large-scale population transfer and exchange.

5. The League of Nations mandate and the more effective United Nations regime of trusteeship. These regimes, in principle at least, deterred the more radical forms of interference with the interests of the colonial peoples associated with colonialism.

The historical experience in New Zealand appears not to conform with any of these standard types. The Maori were not left outside citizenship.[4] Settlement from outside took place lawfully, on the basis of the Treaty of Waitangi.[5] Moreover, whilst the law was often

[4] Art. 3 of the English version of the Treaty of Waitangi 'impart[ed]' to Maori 'all the Rights and Privileges of British subjects'. By the Maori version of the article they were given 'the same rights and duties of citizenship as the people of England'. See Sir Hugh Kawharu's reconstruction of the literal translation, n. 8 below. The status of Maori as British subjects was declared and clarified by the Native Rights 1865 (NZ). Later general nationality and citizenship legislation (see now the Citizenship Act 1977) has applied to them as to Pakeha. See further Ch. 2, n. 4.

[5] The preamble 'legitimised the transmigration of settlers from the United Kingdom': Walker, *Ka Whawhai Tonu Matou*, 99. To enable their settlement, the exclusive right of 'pre-emption' of land was acquired by the Crown under Art. 2 of the Treaty. See e.g. R. Ross, 'Te Tiriti o Waitangi: Texts and Translations', (1972) 6 *NZ Jo. Hist.* 129 at 143–52; R. J. Walker in I. H. [Sir Hugh] Kawharu (ed.), *Waitangi: Māori and Pākehā Perspectives of the Treaty of*

abused, the principle of legality was recognized in relation to land transfers. No doubt there was a serious gap between principle and performance, but the retrospective enforcement of the Treaty of Waitangi,[6] hesitant and partial though it may be, is further evidence of adherence to the principle of legality in the sphere of land transfer.[7]

Waitangi (Auckland, 1989), 265; Orange, *Treaty*, 1, 36–7, 42, 47; and see D. V. Williams in Kawharu (ed.), *Waitangi*, 80. Large tracts of land, including (in circumstances substantially to the Crown's grave discredit) the Ngai Tahu people's holding of most of the South Island, passed to the Crown by purchase under this right: see Kawharu, *Maori Land Tenure*, 75; T. O'Regan in Kawharu (ed.), *Waitangi*, 234; and now the *Ngai Tahu Report* (Wai-27, 1991) of the Waitangi Tribunal (see Ch. 4, nn. 2 and 20). The right became statutorily expressed and secured to the Crown by the New Zealand Constitution Act 1852 (UK), section 73, and was formally ended by the repeal of that section by the Statute Law Revision Act 1892 (UK), section 1: but see n. 7 below.

[6] See e.g. the Treaty of Waitangi Act 1975, constituting the Waitangi Tribunal to inquire into and make recommendations to the Crown as to breaches of the principles of the Treaty (not only in respect of land); the State Owned Enterprises Act 1986, section 9 (in effect requiring the Crown in 'corporatizing' state assets to comply with principles of the Treaty); the Treaty of Waitangi (State Enterprises) Act 1988, empowering the Waitangi Tribunal to make binding recommendations in certain circumstances. For the retroactive extension of its jurisdiction back to 1840, see Ch. 4, n. 18 and text, and, for the giving of some effect to its recommendations, see below at nn. 27–46. Generally for the work of the Tribunal, see P. B. Temm, *The Waitangi Tribunal: The Conscience of the Nation* (Auckland, 1990); W. Renwick, *The Treaty Now* (Wellington, 1990, ch. 1; A. Sharp, *Justice and the Māori* (Auckland, 1990), chs. 7 and 8; E. T. Durie and G. S. Orr, 'The Role of the Waitangi Tribunal and the Development of a Bicultural Jurisprudence' (1990) 14 *NZULR* 62. The question of compliance with the Treaty is (by Cabinet Office direction) required to be considered by those involved in preparing legislation. See *Legislative Change: Guidelines on Process and Content*, Report by the Legislation Advisory Committee, revd. edn. (1991), para. 40. (App. D of this Report lists New Zealand statutes, enacted since 1975, which particularly refer 'to the Treaty . . . to the Maori perspective or to Maori interests'.)

[7] Pre-emption or purchase (see n. 5 above) by the Crown, as the legal means of extinguishing Maori customary title, was in effect generally replaced by the operations of the (Maori) Land Court (established in the 1860s, substantially in its present form by the Native Lands Act 1865; see now the Maori Affairs Act 1953). A principal role of the Court has been to convert Maori customary land, held communally, into 'Maori freehold land' (held under common-law individual tenure) which, subject to the now dominant protective jurisdiction of the Court, may thus become available for disposition to Pakeha. See generally Kawharu, *Maori Land Tenure*; and esp. at pp. 15 ff. for his historical comment on the Native Land Court (originally

The principle of legality in this case is represented by the Treaty of Waitangi and to that I shall now turn.

The significance of the Treaty is such that its text and the background must be presented here as an essential part, not merely of the history, but of the relevant evidence in the case.

The text cited is the reconstruction of the literal translation of the Maori text of the Treaty proposed by Sir Hugh Kawharu:[8]

Victoria, the Queen of England, in her concern to protect the chiefs and subtribes of New Zealand and in her desire to preserve their chieftainship and their lands to them and to maintain peace and good order considers it just to appoint an administrator one who will negotiate with the people of New Zealand to the end that their chiefs will agree to the Queen's Government being established over all parts of this land and (adjoining) islands and also because there are many of her subjects already living on this land and others yet to come. So the Queen desires to establish a government so that no evil will come to Maori and European living in a state of lawlessness. So the Queen has appointed me, William Hobson a captain in the Royal Navy to be Governor for all parts of New Zealand (both those) shortly to be received by the Queen and (those) to be received hereafter and presents to the chiefs of the Confederation chiefs of the subtribes of New Zealand and other chiefs these laws set out here.

so called) as 'a veritable engine of destruction for any tribe's tenure of land, anywhere'. A principle of, so to speak, the barest legality was manifested (following Maori 'rebellion') in the extinguishment of customary title by the Crown's confiscation of large areas of land in the North Island, under the New Zealand Settlements Act 1863 (repealed by the Repeals Act 1878, section 3, but with a general saving provision, section 4). Maori claims that the confiscations (the raupatu) were in breach of principles of the Treaty are now before the Waitangi Tribunal. Loss of land through purchase by the Crown, the operations of the Land Court, or through the raupatu, has left the Maori with about 'one million hectares, some 2% of the country, plus a small . . . area under general titles': M. P. K. Sorrenson, 'Giving Better Effect to the Treaty: Some Thoughts for 1990' (1990) 24 *NZ Jo. Hist.* 135, 148.

[8] See Kawharu (ed.), *Waitangi*, 302–1. The texts of the Treaty accepted by Parliament as authoritative are set out in the First Schedule to the Treaty of Waitangi Act 1975 (as substituted by the Treaty of Waitangi Amendment Act 1985, section 4). The Kawharu reconstruction is quoted by Cooke P. in *New Zealand Maori Council* v. *Attorney-General* [1987] 1 NZLR 641 at 662–3.

The first

The Chiefs of the Confederation and all the chefs who have not joined that Confederation give absolutely to the Queen of England for ever the complete government over their land.

The second

The Queen of England agrees to protect the chiefs, the subtribes and all the people of New Zealand in the unqualified exercise of their chieftainship over their lands, villages and all their treasures. But on the other hand the Chiefs of the Confederation and all the Chiefs will sell land to the Queen at a price agreed to by the person owning it and by the person buying it (the latter being) appointed by the Queen as her purchase agent.

The third

For this agreed arrangement therefore concerning the Government of the Queen, the Queen of England will protect all the ordinary people of New Zealand and will give them the same rights and duties of citizenship as the people of England.

(Signed) W. Hobson
Consul and Lieutenant-Governor

So we, the Chiefs of the Confederation and of the subtribes of New Zealand meeting here at Waitangi having seen the shape of these words which we accept and agree to record our names and our marks thus.

Was done at Waitangi on the sixth of February in the year of our Lord 1840.

There was only one Maori version of the Treaty, and this was signed by most of the chiefs who were party to the Treaty.[9] Some signatures were attached to a copy in English at Waikato Heads.[10]

[9] See further Ch. 2, n. 2 and text. The confederation of chiefs referred to in the Treaty had been established in the north of the country in 1835 at the instigation of the British Resident, James Busby, but had not got much beyond a declaration of independence (which contained a rudimentary constitution) and the designation of a flag. See Orange, *Treaty*, ch. 2; Sinclair, *History*, 51–2; Walker, *Ka Whawhai Tonu Matou*, 88–9. For the text of the Declaration of Independence of the United Tribes of New Zealand (i.e. the confederation just mentioned), see *Facsimiles of the Declaration of Independence and the Treaty of Waitangi* (Wellington, 1877, repr. 1960); Orange, *Treaty*, App. 1, 255–6.

[10] At the mouth of the Waikato River. See Orange, *Treaty*, 69–70.

The significance of the Treaty, as going beyond the merely legal and as forming a part of the mana of the Maori people, is well understood. At the same time, it is important to examine it though the eyes of a lawyer, and to analyse its role and legal significance. First, it is necessary to examine the status of the parties. In 1840 Great Britain was in an early imperial phase and expansion was fairly casual. In the first half of the nineteenth century it was entirely normal for European States, and others, to make treaties with tribal societies. Treaties were made with individual Somali and West African chiefs. In the Pacific region Great Britain made treaties with the King of Hawaii, otherwise known as the Sandwich Islands (1843, 1846, 1851).[11] If there was anything exceptional about the Treaty of Waitangi it was the fact that there was no king or single paramount chief but an acephalous confederation of chiefs and sub-tribes.[12] As a result the formal mechanics of treaty-making were cumbersome.

There can be no doubt, however, that the Treaty of Waitangi presupposed the legal and political capacity of the chiefs of New Zealand to make an agreement which was valid on the international plane. Moreover, there is evidence that, in the decade prior to the conclusion of the Treaty, the British Government conducted itself on the basis that relations with the Maori tribes were governed by the rules of international law.[13] In any event, the British regarded Waitangi as a real treaty and it appears in authoritative collections such as the *British and Foreign State Papers* and *Hertslet's Commercial Treaties*. Moreover, the fact that *subsequent* developments in international law doctrine denied treaty-making capacity to what were described as

[11] *British and Foreign State Papers*, xxxi. 1029–35; xxxiv. 22–3; xl. 71–8, respectively.

[12] See n. 9 above.

[13] H. A. Smith, *Great Britain and the Law of Nations* (London, 1932), i. 30–3.

'Native Chiefs and Peoples' is irrelevant.[14] Facts have to be appreciated according to the principles of international law prevailing at the material time.

The next question is, what was the meaning of the Treaty? From the British point of view it was a treaty of cession, allowing for settlement and for the purchase of land. However, there were reciprocal promises. In particular, the chiefs were promised 'the unqualified exercise of their chieftainship over their lands, villages and all their treasures'. In other words, the chiefs were guaranteed protection of tino rangatiratanga.[15] They were also promised equal citizenship.[16]

There are important questions concerning the interpretation of the Treaty, but its validity is recognized on all sides. For practical purposes, this means that the validity of the Treaty involves a paradox. Its execution meant that the separate international identity of the Confederation of Chiefs was extinguished and the procedure of implementation of the reciprocal promises was transferred from the plane of international law to the plane of internal public law. On this basis the outlook was not promising. The public law principles

[14] Cf. Lord McNair, *The Law of Treaties* (Oxford, 1961), 52–4.

[15] See Art. 2 of the Maori version, and the Kawharu translation of it above. A recurring theme in recent writing (see n. to Preface and Ch. 3, n. 20) is the problem of reconciling the tino rangatiratanga reserved to the chiefs by Art. 2 with the kawanatanga (governance) ceded to the Crown by Art. 1. Contrast with the latter term the 'sovereignty' of the English version and the sovereignty claimed by the New Zealand Crown in Parliament (n. 17 below). For some only of the literature, see discussion by several contributors to Kawharu (ed.), *Waitangi*, esp. pp. xvi–xxii (Kawharu), 263–6 (Walker), 292 (Durie), 300 ff. (B. Biggs); Orange, *Treaty*, 40–1, 106, *et passim*; J. Binney in Green (ed.), *Towards 1990*, 26–7; Sharp, *Justice and the Maori*, 132 ff. and pt. 4 ('Justice and Sovereignty') *passim*. For Sir Hugh Kawharu's view of kawanatanga, as accepted by the Waitangi Tribunal (n. 6 above), see its *Report on the Kaituna River Claim* (Wai-4, 1984), 14; for comment on which and other refs., see F. M. Brookfield, 'Sovereignty: The Treaty, the Courts and the Tribunal' [1989] *NZRL Rev.* 292 and in [1990] *NZLJ* 406 at 415. See also Ch. 4, n. 6 and text. Strongly radical views of Maori entitlement to tino rangatiratanga are propounded by most of the writers referred to in Ch. 3, n. 20. See most recently *Te Whakamarama: The Maori Law Bulletin*, 8 (1991), 6–18.

[16] Art. 3. See n. 4 above.

applied by the Privy Council and other courts applying the common law involved the assumption that treaties did not bind the Crown for internal purposes unless they were incorporated by legislation. Otherwise Treaties were acts of State and therefore not even justiciable. Consequently, various treaties of protection in fact provided no protection against the invasion of the land and other rights of the indigenous people.

In essence this is still the position in New Zealand today. The framework is parliamentary supremacy,[17] but the result is the same. The Treaty of Waitangi is not enforceable in the New Zealand legal system except by way of statute: see the decision of the Privy Council in *Te Heuheu Tukino* v. *Aotea District Maori Land Board* (1941).[18] The statutory innovations since 1975 affecting land rights[19] and natural resources[20] make no difference.

[17] The New Zealand Parliament has full legislative power under (now) the Constitution Act 1986 (NZ) which, in New Zealand law (*a*) replaced the much amended New Zealand Constitution Act 1852 (UK) and the 'independence legislation' of the United Kingdom Parliament (the Statute of Westminster 1931, adopted by New Zealand in 1947, and the New Zealand Constitution Amendment Act 1947); and (*b*) formally terminated the latter Parliament's residual but long disused power to legislate for New Zealand. The theoretical constitutional position of the New Zealand Parliament now approximates, Treaty of Rome complications aside, to that of its United Kingdom parent so that problems of entrenchment are similar. As to those and related problems in the New Zealand context, see e.g. F. M. Brookfield (1984) 5 *OL Rev.* 603; J. B. Elkind (1987) 50 *MLR* 158; and, specifically in relation to the Treaty, P. G. McHugh in Kawharu (ed.), *Waitangi*, 42 ff., and D. V. Williams, 'The Constitutional Status of the Treaty of Waitangi . . .' (1990) 14 *NZULR* 9 at 18 ff. (and Sir Robin Cooke's comments thereon, 14 *NZULR* 1 at 6).

[18] [1941] NZLR 590; [1941] AC 308. See also *New Zealand Maori Council* v. *Attorney-General* [1987] 1 NZLR 641 at 667–8 (Cooke P.); and (generally as to parliamentary sovereignty in relation to the Treaty) at 690 (Somers J.) (cf. *Kaihau* v. *Inland Revenue Department* [1990] 3 NZLR 344). Subject to the *Te Heuheu Tukino* principle, the Treaty is binding (though not as an *international* treaty: see text following n. 61 below) on the Crown in right of New Zealand but no longer on the Crown in right of the United Kingdom. Cf. *R.* v. *Secretary of State, ex parte Indian Association of Alberta* [1982] *QB* 892.

[19] See n. 6 above.

[20] See the Maori Fisheries Act 1989 and (thereon) n. 46 and text; and the Resource Management Act 1991 (cf. n. 38). And cf. R. P. Boast, 'The Treaty of Waitangi: A Framework for Resource Management Law' (1989) 19 *VUWLR*, Mono. 1.

Unless there is some entrenchment of the principles of the Treaty, the legislation can be repealed.[21]

There are, of course, certain other possibilities in the internal law sphere. Professor Brookfield has referred to the possible development of a constitutional convention that Parliament may not legislate contrary to the principles of the Treaty of Waitangi, and the recognition of such a convention by the courts.[22] There is also the view that the concept of common-law aboriginal title has significance, in Paul McHugh's words, as 'the only recognized cause of action independent of statutory concession.[23] However, such possibilities are all, in various ways, problematical.

At this point the essential step would appear to be the statutory incorporation of the principles of the

[21] Entrenchment (see n. 17 above) of the principles of the Treaty (see n. 25 below) was provided for in the Bill of Rights which was tentatively proposed by Government White Paper in 1985 but abandoned in favour of an unentrenched Bill which makes no mention of the Treaty. See further Ch. 4, nn. 28 and 29, and text.

[22] In Brookfield, 'Sovereignty', 294 (n. 15 above), following McHugh's suggestion (Kawharu (ed.), *Waitangi*, 42–4, 49) to the effect that a convention of the Crown's consulting Maori (and obtaining some agreement) about proposed legislation on Maori affairs may be developing. The difficulties in the way of a modern constitutional convention's 'crystallizing' into law are indeed great: see *Re Resolution to Amend the Constitution* [of Canada] [1981] 1 SCR 753, 125 DLR (3*d*)1; but see also *R.* v. *Secretary of State ex parte Indian Association of Alberta* [1982] QB 892 at 937 (judgment of Lord Denning MR implicitly approved by the House of Lords, in refusing leave to appeal), and *Manuel* v. *Attorney-General* [1983] Ch. 77 at 89–94 (Megarry VC).

[23] See McHugh in Kawharu (ed.), *Waitangi*, 53, on whose work the recent renaissance of the common-law doctrine in New Zealand has to a substantial extent depended. See *Te Weehi* v. *Regional Fisheries Officer* [1986] 1 NZLR 680 (distinguished however in *Green* v. *Ministry of Agriculture and Fisheries* [1990] 1 NZLR 411) and the cases cited in n. 45 below; and see the McHugh citations in [1986] 1 NZLR at 691–2 and n. to Preface. A provisionally favourable view of *Te Weehi* and the cases last referred to was expressed, *obiter*, by the Court of Appeal in *Te Runanga o Muriwhenua* v. *Attorney-General* [1990] 2 NZLR 641 at 654–5. See also (*a*) *The Treaty of Waitangi and Maori Fisheries*, New Zealand Law Commission Preliminary Paper 9 (1989) (includes general treatment of the doctrine); (*b*) Boast, 'Treaty Rights or Aboriginal Rights?', [1990] *NZLJ* 32, and (*c*) Ch. 4, n. 19. For recent, brief, summarizing comment see F. M. Brookfield, 'Maori Rights and Two Radical Writers' [1990] *NZLJ* 406, and in Kawharu (ed.), *Waitangi*, 10–12. For full examination of the doctrine in the various jurisdictions, K. McNeil, *Common Law Aboriginal Title* (Oxford, 1989).

Treaty of Waitangi into the law of New Zealand, preferably in the form of an entrenched Bill of Rights.[24] Let us suppose that is achieved. No doubt it would be regarded as an enormous boost to the cause of land claims, and the political importance of such a development is self-evident; but in the practical world what would be achieved? The text of the original Treaty is brief and it is by no means easy to deduce precise principles from its provisions.[25] The Treaty or the relevant part of a Bill of Rights would beg many questions, and might produce less than decisive results. Moreover, the issue of incorporation of the Treaty, like the present internal debate, distracts attention from other, no less effective approaches.

My particular concern is to point out that certain standard-setting conventions concerning human rights are highly relevant to the debate and would probably provide a more positive basis for decision-making than the Treaty of Waitangi. This is not a retrograde position. The presently fashionable approach is to seek to establish 'the principles of the Treaty of Waitangi' rather than to apply the Treaty provisions as such, and this is not entirely surprising. The regime of land alienation provided for in Article 2 was obscure, and, in so far as it was discernible, was discriminatory. The right of pre-emption applied to one race only. Moreover, even the lawful operation of the Treaty was bound to lead to trouble since, in terms of cumulative effect, the individual acts of alienation eroded and disrupted tribal areas and could involve the alienation of communal sites, such as marae.

[24] See n. 21 above.

[25] See text and quotations at nn. 48–52 below. It is the 'principles' of the Treaty that the Waitangi Tribunal (see n. 6 above) gives effect to under the Treaty of Waitangi Act 1975, section 6. For the inclusion of the 'principles' in statute, see also the Environment Act 1986, long title; the Conservation Act 1987, section 4; and the Education Act 1989, section 181 (b).

The Treaty itself is, in any event, too abrupt as an instrument for careful change. As Sir Hugh Kawharu has said, 'Inherent in the simplicity of the Treaty is its lack of a conceptual framework that could accommodate the two cultures . . . and an administrative infrastructure for devising coherent policies and programmes that balance obligations of sovereignty against those of rangatiratanga. There are, indeed, eternal verities in the Treaty, but they will be reduced to mere cant unless they are monitored and fashioned to meet the legitimate demands of the day'.[26]

The truth of this appreciation is confirmed by the character of the claims presented to the Waitangi Tribunal in the period 1983–8. It will be useful to catalogue each claim together with the response of the Crown to the recommendations of the Waitangi Tribunal,[27] largely as reported by the Parliamentary Commissioner for the Environment in November 1988 (with allowance for some later developments):

1. Motunui Claim[28]

The Tribunal found that the traditional fishing grounds of Te Atiawa had been polluted (by sewage and other wastes) and would probably be polluted further, prejudicially affecting the fishing rights guaranteed under the Treaty. The Tribunal recommended that the planned

[26] Kawharu (ed.), *Waitangi*, p. x.

[27] See *Environmental Management and the Principles of the Treaty of Waitangi: Report on Crown Response to the Recommendations of the Waitangi Tribunal*, Nov. 1988 (henceforth *Report on Crown Response*), from which the findings and recommendations of the Tribunal (in its respective reports), and action taken to give effect to the latter, are summarized. Instances of further such action, taken since the Parliamentary Commissioner reported, are indicated below in text or notes. No complete account, or survey of the adequacy, of these later steps (including those in the legislation referred to in nn. 38 and 41 below) is attempted here.

[28] *Report . . . of the Waitangi Tribunal on an Application by Aila Taylor . . . on behalf of Te Atiawa Tribe . . .* (Motunui Report: Wai-6), 1983).

Motunui outfall should not be built, that the existing Waitara outfall should be upgraded, and that legislation should be amended to protect Maori fishing rights.[29]

Five and a half years after the Crown received the Tribunal's recommendations, the Motunui outfall had not been built, but the Waitara reefs continued to be polluted, and the legislation, policy, and practices at fault had not been remedied.

After the Tribunal recommendations were made, the Crown convened a Task Force of officials who carried out a number of investigations. The final recommendation to the Crown was to construct a new long outfall at Waitara with the intention that treatment of effluent would follow at a later stage and be the responsibility of the companies and local authorities involved. This outcome was not regarded as satisfactory in all quarters. The Parliamentary Commissioner for the Environment reported to Parliament in July 1988 that:[30]

> My inquiries have not established all causes for the delays in the parties' reaching agreement. However, I believe the decision by the Ministry of Energy to negotiate the Heads of Agreement through its trading arm . . . contributed to protracted negotiations.
>
> To achieve satisfactory effluent discharge standards through the Waitara outfall requires far greater commitment and persistence by the Ministry of Energy and the North Taranaki District Council than has been shown so far.

The Ombudsmen reported to Parliament in 1988 that[31] 'the sum total of the delays which have occurred and which continue to occur in achieving a result, render all arguments rationalising them untenable'.

[29] See summary in the *Report on Crown Response*, 9, 11.

[30] Quoted ibid. 11.

[31] Quoted ibid. Some progress has been made since, in the passing of the Maori Fisheries Act 1989 (n. 46 below) and the Resource Management Act 1991 (cf. n. 38 below); and in the construction of the new outfall now in use.

2. Kaituna Claim[32]

The Tribunal found that plans to re-route Rotorua sewage by pipeline to the Kaituna River would prejudicially affect Ngati Pikiao by polluting their traditional fishing grounds. The Tribunal recommended that the 'nutrient pipeline' plans should be abandoned and alternatives found, and that deficient legislation be changed.[33]

Those recommendations related to the Kaituna pipeline had been implemented or were in the process of being implemented by the end of 1988. Recommendations relating to legislation had not been implemented, with the exception of one recommendation which was covered by the proposed resource management law reform.[34]

3. Manukau Claim[35]

The Tribunal found that the tribes of the Manukau Harbour had been severely prejudiced in their enjoyment of traditional lands and fisheries through compulsory acquisitions, land and industrial developments, reclamations, waste discharges, zonings, commercial fishing, and the denial of traditional harbour access, contrary to the guarantees under the Treaty. The Tribunal recommended changes to legislation and Crown policy, an action plan to clean up the harbour

[32] *Report of the Waitangi Tribunal on the Kaituna River Claim* (Wai-4, 1984). The Ngati Pikiao people, upon whose behalf the claim was brought, are a hapu (sub-tribe) of Te Arawa, a group of tribes of the central part of the North Island.

[33] See summary in *Report on Crown Response*, 11.

[34] A new treatment plant is now in use. The legislative matters are dealt with at least in part by the Resource Management Act 1991 (cf. n. 38 below).

[35] *Finding of the Waitangi Tribunal on the Manukau Claim* (Wai-8, 1985).

and restore its mana with participation of tangata whenua, and return of certain lands and fisheries.[36]

While the Crown had in some way addressed (at least in part) most of the Manukau recommendations, three years after those recommendations were issued none of them had been sufficiently implemented to show any real change 'at the flaxroots level'. Understandably, the claimants felt frustration and cynicism, and had made their concerns known in the national media and in international forums. When not acting on Tribunal recommendations, the Crown had neglected to explain how the problems identified by the Tribunal would be solved by its chosen approach.

Some of the recommendations involved significant changes to current environmental management, particularly Recommendation 3 concerning the restoration of the Manukau Harbour. While a Manukau Harbour Strategy has been completed as recommended, implementation will take many years and the co-operation of some twenty agencies, and it will take years before the restorative effects of present changes will be seen.

Recommendations 2 and 6 (exclusive fisheries) would have provided interim relief to claimants until the health of the harbour's ecosystem had been restored. They would have required relatively little administrative effort to implement.[37]

Recommendations requiring legislative change (1, 7, 8, and 13) remain outstanding, but these may be covered in current reviews of resource management and local authority legislation.[38]

[36] See summary in *Report on Crown Response*, 12.

[37] Steps that were taken have been to some extent superseded by the claimants' application for fishing rights, in respect of the Manukau Harbour, made under the Taiapure–Local Fisheries provisions of the Maori Fisheries Act 1989, section 74 (inserting a new Part IIIA in the Fisheries Act 1983).

[38] These numbered recommendations related respectively to (*inter alia*) (1) the Crown's fiduciary responsibilities to Maori in respect of rivers, harbours, the foreshore, etc.; (7) the reform of planning and water and soil control legislation to give effect to Treaty principles; (8) funding to enable

4. Orakei Claim[39]

The Tribunal found that the Crown, through acts and omissions contrary to the Treaty, caused Ngati Whatua to be virtually landless. The Tribunal recommended that certain lands be returned and a tribal endowment be granted to assist in tribal rehabilitation. The Tribunal also referred to the Attorney-General a consideration of pardons and remissions of fines for the protesters who sought to bring these injustices to the attention of the Crown.[40] The Crown accepted all those Tribunal recommendations directed to Ministers, but the Attorney-General disagreed with the Tribunal's assessment of matters referred to him.

The tribal endowment had been paid, and the legislative amendments required to implement the majority of the recommendations were being drafted and were expected to be introduced shortly.[41]

During the ten months that elapsed between the lodging of the recommendations with Ministers and payment of the endowment to Ngati Whatua, the Treaty Issues Unit in the Department of Maori Affairs was actively pursuing resolution of the recommendations as a priority issue.

tribal authorities to establish an 'economic base'; and (13) protection of wahi tapu. (See the Tribunal's *Finding . . . on the Manukau Claim*, 129–34). See the Resource Management Act 1991, which to some extent covers nos. (1), (7), and (13).

[39] *Report of the Waitangi Tribunal on the Orakei Claim* (Wai-9, 1987). The claim had been brought on behalf of the Ngati Whatua people, from whom the Crown acquired the original site of the City of Auckland in 1840, in respect of the later losses to the Crown of virtually all their remaining land. See, as well as the Tribunal's Report *passim*, Walker, *Ka Whawhai Tonu Matou*, 215–19 and (for background legal detail) F. M. Brookfield, 'Protest and Possession at Bastion Point' [1978] *NZLJ* 383.

[40] See summary in *Report on Crown Response*, 13.

[41] See the Orakei Bill now (1 Sept. 1991) before Parliament.

5. Muriwhenua Claim[42]

The Tribunal found that the Treaty guaranteed the ownership of fisheries to Maori in the same way as land, and the Crown assumption of control over the fisheries without prior negotiation with Maori was contrary to the Treaty. The Tribunal recommended that current negotiations between Crown and Maori on fisheries be continued in good faith, and the costs of Maori negotiators be met by the Crown. In relation to land, the Tribunal had recommended that transfers of Crown land to state-owned enterprises should not be made until Maori interests in the land could be protected.[43]

The Crown response to the interim report on transfer of Crown land to state-owned enterprises was prompt, and resulted in the *Maori Council* case coming before the Court of Appeal.[44] The Crown response to the two subsequent memoranda on the Individual Transferable Quota fishing system was nil, until forced by restraining orders from the High Court.[45] Negotiations took place between the Crown and Maori, but did not reach agreement. The Maori Fisheries Bill introduced in September 1988 contained some matters agreed upon between parties, but also went much further in introducing matters not under negotiation (that is, freshwater fisheries), proposing a restrictive allocation of

[42] *Report of the Waitangi Tribunal on the Muriwhenua Fishing Claim* (Wai-22, 1988). The land issues associated with the Muriwhenua claim had been the subject of an interim report which resulted in the *Maori Council* case [1987] 1 NZLR 641. See text below. The claim was made on behalf of tribes in the Far North of the country, collectively known as Muriwhenua. See, as well as the Tribunal's Report *passim*, Walker, *Ka Whawhai Tonu Matou*, 273–7.

[43] See summary in *Report on Crown Response*, 14.

[44] *New Zealand Maori Council* v. *Attorney-General* [1987] 1 NZLR 641.

[45] *New Zealand Maori Council and Runanga o Muriwhenua* v. *Attorney-General* (1987, Greig J.) See also the (in effect) extension of the order to fishing claims of other tribes in *Ngai Tahu Maori Trust Board* v. *Attorney-General* (1987, Greig J.) Both judgments are set out in App. 5 to the *Report on the Muriwhenua Fishing Claim*. See further n. 23 above as to provisionally favourable Court of Appeal comment.

quota, and, most significantly, proposing that Maori rights of access to Courts and the Waitangi Tribunal in regard to fisheries be taken away.

The Crown's final proposals, mentioned in part by the Parliamentary Commissioner in her Report and given effect since in the Maori Fisheries Act 1989, fixed the total Maori quota share at 10 per cent (in contrast to the 50 per cent share, to have been acquired over twenty years, as previously proposed) retaining however Maori access to Courts and Tribunal that would enable further consideration of Treaty and common law fishing rights.[46]

It is clear that what is involved is a fairly complex balancing of interests involving control of the environment as well as entitlements. Moreover, the issues of entitlement are not ordinary questions of individual ownership but involve major issues of public law. A necessary consequence of this is the appearance of cross-claims by other tribal claimants.[47]

The Treaty provisions as such are not much help. Nor from a rigorous standpoint are the principles of the Treaty of Waitangi as defined by the Waitangi Tribunal. They are, of course, much better than nothing, but they are characterized by an unsatisfying generality. They have been summarized recently as follows:[48]

1. The exchange of the right to make laws for the obligation to protect Maori interests.

[46] For an analysis of the Act, see D. V. Williams, 'Maori Issues II' [1990] *NZRL Rev.* 129 at 132–4. Williams quotes (ibid. 134) Cooke P.'s description of the Act as in effect an 'interim measure' only, in *Te Runanga o Muriwhenua* v. *Attorney-General* [1990] 2 NZLR 641, 649–50.

[47] As in relation to the Ngai Tahu claim recently determined by the Tribunal. See the *Ngai Tahu Report* (Wai-27, 1991), i. 1, 23, 25.

[48] *Report on Crown Response*, 104. See further n. 25 above. Cf. the Government's somewhat similar statement of *Principles of Crown Action on the Treaty of Waitangi* (Wellington, 1989) which however includes the principle of redress not expressly mentioned in the Parliamentary Commissioner's summary. The Government's statement drew strong radical criticism: see e.g. D. V. Williams, 'Crown Action on the Treaty of Waitangi' (1990) 2 *Ab. LB* 12.

2. The Treaty implies a partnership, exercised with utmost good faith.
3. The Treaty is an agreement that can be adapted to meet new circumstances.
4. The needs of both Maori and the wider community must be met, which will require compromises on both sides.
5. The Maori interest should be actively protected by the Crown.
6. The Crown cannot evade its obligations under the Treaty by conferring authority on some other body.
7. The principle that traditional mechanisms for tribal controls would continue to be respected and maintained.
8. Tino rangatiratanga in the Treaty includes management of resources and other taonga according to Maori cultural preferences.
9. The principle that the Maori has an effective option either to follow a traditional cultural pattern or to accept cultural assimilation, or to adopt a pattern involving tribal ways and a more individualistic style.

It is a striking fact that the Waitangi Tribunal has found it necessary to propound a principle which involves a creative interpretation of Article 2 of the Treaty of Waitangi. Thus in the Report on the Orakei Claim the Tribunal stated the position in the following way:[49]

> It is abundantly evident . . . that Lord Normanby, in instructing Captain Hobson to obtain for the Crown the right of the pre-emption of Maori land, and in stipulating how such right was to be exercised, made it clear that no land was to be so purchased which was needed to provide for the comfort and subsistence of the Maori people. In short, they

[49] *Report . . . on the Orakei Claim*, 144, 147.

were to be left with a sufficient endowment for their own needs. An official protector was to ensure this. The right of pre-emption was to be a limited right. It was not to extend to land needed by the Maori . . . we find that Article 2, read as a whole, imposed on the Crown certain duties and responsibilities, the first to ensure that the Maori people in fact wished to sell; the second to ensure that they were left with sufficient land for their maintenance and support or livelihood or, as Chief Judge Durie puts it in the Waiheke Report . . . that each tribe maintained a sufficient endowment for its foreseen needs.

It is of interest to compare the principles propounded by the Waitangi Tribunal with those formulated by the Court of Appeal in the *New Zealand Maori Council* case decided in 1987. The principles were not formulated *as such*, it should be emphasized, but appear in the course of interpretation of the phrase 'principles of the Treaty of Waitangi' in a statute. The key formulation, stated in the words of President Cooke, was, 'the principles . . . require the Pakeha and Maori Treaty partners to act towards each other reasonably and with the utmost good faith.'[50] The other principles stated by members of the Court of Appeal were essentially corollaries of the concept of a bargain between two identified parties in which the acquisition of sovereignty was exchanged for certain guarantees given to the Maori, these guarantees involving, in broad terms, the 'protection' of the Crown. This more or less fiduciary duty on the part of the Crown[51] was stated to be the counterpart of a duty

[50] *New Zealand Maori Council* v. *Attorney-General* [1987] 1 NZLR 641 at 667.

[51] Cf. the fiduciary obligations of the Crown to indigenous peoples more precisely laid down in Canada (and now strengthened by the Constitution Act 1982, section 35 (1)) by the Supreme Court in *Guerin* v. *The Queen* [1984] 2 SCR 335, 13 DLR (4th) 321; for favourable discussion of which see Cooke P. (delivering the judgment of the Court of Appeal) in *Te Runanga o Muriwhenua* v. *Attorney-General* [1990] 2 NZLR 641, 655. See also McNeil, *Common Law Aboriginal Title*, 284–8 and, now, *R.* v. *Sparrow* (1990) 70 DLR (4th) 385 (SCC).

on the part of the Maori people to provide 'reasonable cooperation'.[52]

The work both of the Waitangi Tribunal and of the Court of Appeal should not be underestimated, and it is facile always to criticize judges *both* for not going far enough *and* for legislating. The judges have had to make the best of the very spare provisions of the Treaty.

But the point is that there are other sources of assistance and that more or less exclusive focus on the Treaty provisions is a conservative and unnecessarily inhibiting factor in law-finding. In the first place, there are contemporary standards of human rights which should be relevant to the interpretation and application of New Zealand legislation, including the provisions which incorporate the principles of the Treaty of Waitangi. No doubt the use of such treaty standards is difficult in the absence of express statutory incorporation,[53] but the New Zealand as well as the English Courts have shown an ability to take treaty obligations into account in the process of statutory interpretation even in the absence of incorporation. Both in the United Kingdom and in New Zealand there is a presumption that the intention of Parliament was to avoid collision with the international obligations of the Crown.[54]

There is also the probability that at least certain standards and principles of human rights have crystallized as rules of customary international law.[55] The consequence of this would be that they would be a part of the law of New Zealand except in cases of incompatibility with an express statutory provision.

There is thus a body of external rules and legal experience which must surely be an important aid to

[52] [1987] 1 NZLR 641 at 664.
[53] Ch. 4, n. 37 and text.
[54] See Ch. 4, n. 38 and text.
[55] See Ch. 4, n. 41 and text.

the interpretation and application of the Treaty of Waitangi and related legislation.

It should be pointed out that there are important human rights instruments to which New Zealand has become a party. The principal sources of treaty obligations for present purposes are four major standard-setting treaties: first, two Covenants which form a general code of human rights, namely the International Covenant on Civil and Political Rights and the International Covenant on Economic, Social and Cultural Rights.[56] Whilst the Government has made certain reservations, these do not impinge on the rights or interests of the Maori. Of particular significance is the fact that recently New Zealand adhered to the Optional Protocol to the International Covenant on Civil and Political Rights.[57] This provides that a State Party to the Protocol recognizes the competence of the Human Rights Committee (created by the Covenant) to receive communications from individuals subject to its jurisdiction who claim to be victims of a violation by the State Party of any of the rights set forth in the Covenant. The main condition placed upon this right of individual recourse is that the complainant must have exhausted all available domestic remedies. (In passing, it may be asked whether the procedure in the Waitangi Tribunal counts as a 'domestic remedy' for this purpose.)

Secondly, New Zealand has become party to two other important standard-setting conventions, both concerned with the principle of equality. They are the International Convention on the Elimination of All Forms of Racial Discrimination[58] and the Convention on the Elimination of All Forms of Discrimination Against Women.[59] Other human rights conventions to

[56] *Multilateral Treaties in Respect of which the Secretary-General Performs Depositary Functions: List of Signatures, Ratifications, Accessions, etc., as at 31 December 1989*, 123, 134.

[57] Ibid. 162. [58] Ibid. 106. [59] Ibid. 170.

which New Zealand has become a party are less relevant here.

In examining how these developments relate to the Treaty of Waitangi, there are some issues of general principle to consider. These instruments involve the existing international obligations of New Zealand and contain detailed provisions on various issues to which the Treaty is supposed to be applicable. It would be reasonable to apply the principles of Waitangi in the light of New Zealand's current commitment to human rights standards in the sphere of treaty obligations, and to ask whether they would result in the enhancement of the Treaty of Waitangi or in its subversion. In principle the Treaty of Waitangi would be much enhanced. The international conventions contain provisions, especially in respect of racial discrimination, which would provide increased legal protection for any racial group not having a dominant position in the political system of New Zealand. In particular, they are likely to provide protection in respect of the use of the language of the group in schools and in other contexts.

In other respects the human rights standards imposed by the conventions will apply without qualification to each and every community. Patterns of conduct which involve, for example, discrimination against women, and which are recognized or maintained in the legal system or in administrative practice, will fall foul of the international standard against discrimination. This will be so whatever the cultural origins of the discrimination. Moreover, the Convention on the Elimination of All Forms of Discrimination Against Women adopts the normal policy of imposing a duty on State parties 'to adopt legislative and other measures, including sanctions where appropriate, prohibiting all discrimination against women', and, further, 'to establish legal protection of the rights of women on an equal basis with men and to ensure through competent tribunals and other public institutions the effective protection of women against any act of discrimination' (Article 2).

The application of the international standards to the issue of land titles is obviously a question of major importance. It is also a question of some difficulty. The issue of historical equity, that is to say, of restitution in accordance with the Treaty of Waitangi Act, is not one which can be easily related to the usual formulations of human rights standards.

In a general way the principle of fairness in land transfer, which is contained in the Treaty itself and assumed in the Act of 1975, is reflected in the principle of non-discrimination which forms a significant element in the international conventions. However, the modern instruments do not relate to the particular problem of historical equity and it is not easy to forecast to what extent a creative use of the concept of equality would produce a justification for the revision of land titles. Moreover, there is room for the view that contemporary standards of human rights would impose certain limitations on the revision of current land titles where this would involve the disturbance of existing occupiers of property without a proportionate gain for the Maori group involved in the claim.

A prevailing concept in contemporary human rights law is that of proportionality: that is to say, that the change proposed, or the measure which is challenged, on human rights grounds must not entail effects not reasonably necessary to the attainment of the purpose in view.[60] The question of relating the principles of the Treaty of Waitangi to the standards prescribed in the international conventions will be examined further in the second and third lectures.

[60] *Belgian Linguistics* case, Judgment on the Merits, 23 July 1968, *Publications of the European Court of Human Rights*, ser. A, no. 6, pp. 34, 44, 70, 86–7; 45 ILR 165, 174, 200, 216–17.

For the while I need to turn to a different aspect of this relationship, namely, the extent to which the New Zealand Courts may refer to the treaty obligations of the Crown in New Zealand in the course of applying the Treaty of Waitangi. For the non-lawyers I should explain that the Courts do not apply the treaty obligations of the Crown unless they have been incorporated by Statute.[61] The basis of this need for incorporation lies in constitutional law. If the Crown could change the law simply by the making of a treaty this would encroach on the sovereignty of Parliament. There is, however, a certain grey area, and the Courts may refer to treaties and conventions, even if they have not been incorporated in legislation, in the course of interpreting legislation.

At this point a remarkable anomaly is encountered. The Treaty of Waitangi does not fit into the normal pattern, that is, of external treaty obligations, some of which are and some of which are not incorporated into legislation. In the first place, it is not binding upon the Crown as a valid *international* treaty: for New Zealand it is not a treaty in force. Its result was the disappearance of one of the international persons involved in the transaction. Consequently the Treaty does not have the same legal status *in public international law terms* as the recent international conventions concerning human rights. However, the internal relations of the Treaty are very similar to those of a currently valid international agreement. Its enforceability depends upon statutory recognition of the rights protected by its provisions.

Of course, a certain level of statutory recognition has been given to the Treaty, in particular in the legislation of 1975. In this way yet another perspective opens up. If and when there is legislation expressly incorporating the human rights conventions to which New Zealand is

[61] See Ch. 4, n. 37.

a party it may be necessary to resolve discordances between legislation reflecting Waitangi and legislation reflecting the multilateral human rights conventions. In fact, the two International Covenants on Human Rights to which reference was made earlier have been given what may be described as a partial incorporation in the Human Rights Commission Act 1977, the long title of which is, 'An Act to establish a Human Rights Commission and to promote the advancement of human rights in New Zealand *in general accordance* with the United Nations International Covenants on Human Rights.'

The general outcome is that the Treaty of Waitangi must take its place with the other forms of evidence as to the obligations of the Crown in the sphere of racial discrimination and the rights of the different communities. This result involves shifting the emphasis away from Waitangi to some extent, but in fact gives a greater overall emphasis to the standards by which the conduct of government in human rights matters may be judged. In so far as the provisions of the Treaty of Waitangi are not entrenched in the New Zealand legal system, the existence of these other sources of external standards is the more significant. In order to assess them more fully it will be necessary to explore the concept of group rights in the context of public international law, together with the models related to group rights, which include self-determination, the protection of minorities, and the concept of indigenous peoples. This system of topics will be examined in my second and third lectures.

2

The Framework: Group Rights and Self-Determination

In the course of this lecture, the debate focused upon the Treaty of Waitangi will be approached from a different angle, that of group rights. The concept of group rights is reflected in a series of standard political models including self-determination and its analogues, the protection of minorities, and the rights of indigenous peoples. These models will be examined and their current relevance assessed. However, the particular ramifications of the concept of indigenous peoples will be reserved as the subject of the third lecture.

The umbrella concept for present purposes is that of group rights. Oddly enough, it is far from easy to produce a neat definition of group rights. At least two criteria appear to be involved. First, there is the idea that group rights are certain types of individual rights which tend to be exercised as a member of a group, as, for example, the right to enjoy rights without discrimination as to race, colour, and so forth, and the right to freedom of conscience and religion. Secondly, there is the bolder criterion according to which group rights involve elements of recognition of the cultural or other identity of the group, which recognition is not ensured by the normal application of the provisions representing individual rights.

There can be no doubt that the Treaty of Waitangi is to a great extent about the recognition of group rights. It is helpful to re-establish a historical footing at this point, by working back from the Treaty of Waitangi Act 1975. This as originally enacted, defined the jurisdiction of the Tribunal as follows (section 6):

Jurisdiction of Tribunal to consider claims

(1) Where any Maori claims that he or any group of Maoris of which he is a member is or is likely to be prejudicially affected—

(a) By any Act, regulations, or Order in Council, for the time being in force; or

(b) By any policy or practice adopted by or on behalf of the Crown and for the time being in force or by any policy or practice proposed to be adopted by or on behalf of the Crown; or

(c) By any act which, after the commencement of this Act, is done or omitted, or is proposed to be done or omitted, by or on behalf of the Crown,—

and that the Act, regulations, or Order in Council, or the policy, practice, or act is inconsistent with the principles of the Treaty, he may submit that claim to the Tribunal under this section.

The interpretation section (section 2) defines the term 'Maori' to mean 'a person of the Maori race of New Zealand; and includes any descendant of such a person'.

The provisions of the Treaty of Waitangi itself very clearly envisage the conditions of common citizenship of Maori and of European settlers, and its preamble refers to the appointment of an administrator 'who will negotiate with the people of New Zealand', as represented by the chiefs of the Confederation and of the subtribes of New Zealand.[1]

The Treaty was drawn up in haste, and both sides were unhampered by the constraints of professional assistance. Its signature was a cumulative process, with chiefs adding signatures to the Maori text at different locations throughout the islands, a total of over 500

[1] A new section 6 (1), extending the jurisdiction of the Tribunal back to 1840, was substituted by the Treaty of Waitangi Amendment Act 1985, section 3. See Ch. 4, text at n.18.)

signatures being received.[2] No attention was paid to authorizations to sign, to the definition of the land over which the signatories exercised authority, or to the definition of the groups represented by the persons signing. Some important tribes refused to become parties to the Treaty.[3] Nevertheless, in the course of time the Maori people have adopted the Treaty as a charter of their group rights and consequently the rehearsal of the oddities attending its conclusion is probably an academic exercise.[4]

It is relevant at this point to look at the Instructions received by Captain Hobson, the negotiator for the British Crown, from Lord Normanby, the Secretary of State for War and Colonies, dated 14 August 1839.[5] The most significant passages are worth quoting in full:

a very considerable Body of Her Majesty's Subjects have already established their residence and effected Settlements there, and that many persons in this Kingdom have formed themselves into a Society, having for its object the acquisition of Land, and the removal of Emigrants, to those Islands.

Her Majesty's Government have watched these proceedings with attention and solicitude. We have not been insensible

[2] For accounts of the signings and the background thereto, see C. Orange, *The Treaty of Waitangi* (Wellington, 1987), chs. 3 and 4; J. Binney, 'The Maori and the Signing of the Treaty of Waitangi', in D. Green (ed.), *Towards 1990* (Wellington, 1989), 20 ff.

[3] See R. J. Walker, in I. H. Kawharu (ed.), *Waitangi: Māori and Pākehā Perspectives of the Treaty of Waitangi* (Auckland, 1989), 267–8; and Orange, *Treaty*, 60–91.

[4] For the early view (held by the first Attorney-General, William Swainson, in 1842 but rejected by the Imperial Government) that the tribes of chiefs who had not signed the Treaty were not under British sovereignty, see Orange, ibid. 110–11. The status of all Maori as British subjects was declared by the Native Rights Act 1865 (cf. Ch. 1, n. 4). For a recent (unsuccessful) plea that persons descended from members of a non-signatory tribe were not subject to New Zealand statute law, see *Kohu* v. *Police* (1989) 5 CRNZ 194.

[5] Normanby to Hobson; 14, 15 Aug. 1839, CO 209/4, pp. 251–81. See W. D. McIntyre and W. J. Gardner (eds.), *Speeches and Documents on New Zealand History* (Oxford, 1971), 10–13, 14. (Lord Normanby's Instructions were cited in the *New Zealand Maori Council* case, [1987] 1 NZLR at 682 (Richardson J.) and 692–3 (Somers J.).)

to the importance of New Zealand to the Interests of Great Britain in Australia, nor unaware of the great natural resources by which that Country is distinguished, or that its geographical position must in seasons, either of peace or of war, enable it, in the hands of Civilized men to exercise a paramount influence in that quarter of the globe. There is probably no part of the earth in which Colonization could be effected with a greater or surer prospect of national advantage.

On the other hand, the Ministers of the Crown have been restrained by still higher motives from engaging in such an enterprise. They have deferred to the advice of the Committee appointed by the House of Commons in the year 1836, to inquire into the state of the aborigines residing in the vicinity of our Colonial Settlements; and have concurred with that Committee in thinking that the increase of national wealth and power promised by the acquisition of New Zealand, would be a most inadequate compensation for the injury which must be inflicted on this Kingdom itself, by embarking in a measure essentially unjust, and but too certainly fraught with calamity to a numerous and inoffensive people, whose title to the soil and to the Sovereignty of New Zealand is indisputable, and has been solemnly recognised by the British Gov[ernmen]t. We retain these opinions in unimpaired force; and though circumstances entirely beyond our control have at length compelled us to alter our course, I do not scruple to avow that we depart from it with extreme reluctance . . .

The necessity for the interposition of the Gov[ernmen]t has however become too evident to admit of any further inaction. The reports which have reached this Office within the last few months establish the facts that, about the commencement of the year 1838, a Body of not less than two thousand British Subjects had become permanent inhabitants of New Zealand, that amongst them were many persons of bad or doubtful character—convicts who had fled from our penal Settlements, or Seamen who had deserted their Ships; and that these people, unrestrained by any Law, and amenable to no tribunals, were alternately the authors and the victims of every species of Crime and outrage. It further appears that extensive cessions of Land have been obtained from the Natives, and that several hundred persons have recently sailed from this Country to occupy and cultivate those Lands. The spirit of adventure having been thus effectually roused, it can no longer be doubted that an extensive Settlement of British Subjects will be rapidly established in New Zealand; and that, unless protected and restrained by necessary Laws and Institutions, they will repeat, unchecked, in that corner of the Globe, the same process of War and spoliation, under which uncivilized Tribes have almost invariably disappeared as often as they have been brought into the immediate vicinity of Emigrants from the Nations of Christendom. To mitigate, and, if possible, to avert these disasters, and to rescue the Emigrants themselves from the evils of a lawless state of Society, it has been resolved to adopt the most effective measures for establishing amongst them a settled form of Civil Gov[ernmen]t. To accomplish this design is the principal object of your Mission. I have already stated that we acknowledge New Zealand as a Sovereign and independent State, so far at least as it is possible to make that acknowledgement in favour of a people composed of numerous, dispersed, and petty Tribes, who possess few political relations to each other, and are incompetent to act, or even deliberate, in concert. But the admission of their rights, though inevitably qualified by this consideration, is binding on the faith of the British Crown. The Queen, in common with Her Majesty's immediate Predecessor, disclaims for herself and for her Subjects, every pretention to seize on the Islands of New Zealand, or to govern them as a part of the Dominion of Great Britain, unless the free and intelligent consent of the Natives, expressed according to their established usages, shall be first obtained. Believing however that their own welfare would, under the circumstances I have mentioned, be best promoted by the surrender to Her Majesty of a right now so precarious and little more than nominal and persuaded that the benefits of British protection, and of Laws administered by British Judges would far more than compensate for the sacrifice by the Natives of a National independence which they are no longer able to maintain, Her Majesty's Gov[ernmen]t have resolved to authorize you to treat with the Aborigines of New Zealand for the recognition of Her Majesty's Sovereign authority over the whole or any parts of those Islands which they may be willing to place under Her Majesty's Dominion. I am not unaware of the difficulty by which such a Treaty may be encountered. The motives by which it is recommended are of course open to suspicion . . .

It is not however to the mere recognition of the sovereign authority of the Queen that your endeavours are to be confined, or your negociations directed. It is further necessary that the Chiefs should be induced, if possible, to contract with you, as representing Her Majesty, that henceforward no Lands shall be Ceded either gratuitously or otherwise, except to the Crown of Great Britain.

. . . .

All dealings with the Aborigines for their Lands must be conducted on the same principles of sincerity, justice, and good faith as must govern your transactions with them for the recognition of Her Majesty's Sovereignty in the Islands. Nor is this all. They must not be permitted to enter into any Contracts in which they might be the ignorant and unintentional authors of injuries to themselves. You will not, for example, purchase from them any Territory, the retention of which by them would be essential, or highly conducive, to their own comfort, safety or subsistence. The acquisition of Land by the Crown for the future Settlement of British Subjects must be confined to such Districts as the Natives can alienate without distress or serious inconvenience to themselves. To secure the observance of this rule will be one of the first duties of their official protector.

This important and very candid document is often neglected by commentators on the Treaty, and yet it must have probative value for purposes of the interpretation of the Treaty and the Statutes which refer to it, or to its principles.

The subject of the Treaty of Waitangi is, in a sense, that of group rights. In the modern evolution of international law, group rights have been a derivative of human rights. The precise term 'human rights' appears in the public domain for the first time at the San Francisco Conference in 1945 and in various provisions of the United Nations Charter. The actual phrases used refer to 'the principle of equal rights and self-determination of peoples', and to 'respect for human rights and for fundamental freedoms for all without distinction as to race, sex, language, or religion': see Articles 1, 13 55, 56, and 76 (in particular). In addition in the Preamble to the Charter it is declared that, '*We the peoples of the United Nations determined* . . . to reaffirm faith in fundamental human rights, in the dignity and worth of the human person, in the equal rights of men and women and of nations large and small'.

The term 'human rights' in fact appears in the years 1942 to 1944 in the course of internal policy discussions in the United States on the subject of the principles on which the postwar organization would be based. It is obvious that the term 'human rights' is more or less the equivalent of earlier terms, such as the 'Rights of Man', the 'rights' of citizens as set forth in the American Bill of Rights, and the older concept of 'natural rights'.

Since 1945 in the era of the United Nations the concept of human rights has acquired a multilateral sanction, a harder outline, a legitimacy on the international plane. The principles of human rights have emerged as an objective and general international legal standard. The consequence has been that the principles of human rights now constitute a standard which is external to the individual states but also intrusive. In other words domestic legal and social values have now become subject to external tests and evaluation. Even the normal application of national and local legal rules to the citizens of the given state may not be sufficient, if the rules themselves fail to accord with the relevant external standards. Before 1945 the application of what would now be called human rights standards was a matter of political exception. The Covenant of the League of Nations contained no generally applicable principles of this kind. Only in the specialized contexts of mandated territories, and treaty provisions in the peace treaties and minorities treaties of the years 1919 to 1920, were standards imposed.

Inherent in the concepts of equality and of human rights is the idea that groups may have rights as such. The classical human rights instruments say little or nothing about the rights of groups apart from the right of self-determination. However, in the Covenant on Civil and Political Rights[6] the family is stated to be 'the natural and fundamental group unit of society' (Article 23) and Article 27 provides that, 'In those States in which ethnic, religious or linguistic minorities exist, persons belonging to such minorities shall not be denied the right, in community with the other members of their group, to enjoy their own culture, to profess and practise their own religion, or to use their own language.'

In a general way, the assumption lying behind the classical formulations of standards of human rights, including the Universal Declaration of 1948 and the two Covenants of 1966, has been that group rights would be taken care of automatically as the result of the protection of the rights of individuals. Thus, if it is provided that 'everyone shall have the right to freedom of thought, conscience, and religion', then it is to be assumed that the rights of members of a religious community are adequately protected. Moreover, the Covenant on Civil and Political Rights contains a strong guarantee of equality before the law. Article 26 thereof provides that 'the law shall prohibit any

[6] Since the giving of the Robb Lectures New Zealand's 'commitment' to the Covenant has been 'affirm[ed]' by the enactment of the New Zealand Bill of Rights Act 1990: see the long title. The Act is not entrenched (cf. Ch. 1, nn. 17 and 21) and any possibility of the Courts' assuming a power of judicial review to give effect to it is barred by section 4. See further text at Ch. 4, n. 29.

discrimination and guarantee to all persons equal and effective protection against discrimination on any ground such as race, colour, sex, language, religion, political or other opinion, national or social origin, property, birth or other status'.

However, it is not the case that the rights of groups are taken care of in all respects by the protection of the rights of individuals. Certain claims by groups which are not on their face unreasonable have involved subject matters not adequately covered by the usual prescriptions for individuals. Three types of such claims may be identified, although there may be others.

First, the classical formulations do not cope with claims to positive action to maintain the cultural and linguistic identity of communities, especially when the members of the community concerned are to some extent territorially scattered. It is to be recalled that Article 27 of the Civil and Political Rights Covenant, already quoted in regard to the protection of ethnic, religious or linguistic minorities, formulates a classical static guarantee, namely, that such persons 'shall not be denied the right' to enjoy their own culture, and so forth.

The question of positive action was highlighted by the decision of the European Court of Human Rights in the *Belgian Linguistics* case of 1968.[7] In that case six groups of applicants from communities of French-speaking residents of the Flemish part of Belgium were seeking to use Article 2 of the First Protocol to the European Convention in order to increase opportunities for their children to be educated in French, the language of the family. Article 2 provides that: 'No person shall be denied the right to education. In the exercise of any functions which it assumes in relation to education and to teaching the State shall respect the right of parents to ensure such education and teaching

[7] Judgment on the Merits, 23 July 1968, *Publications of the European Court of Human Rights*, ser. A. no. 6; 45 ILR 136.

in conformity with their own religious and philosophical convictions.' One of the complaints presented by the applicants consisted of the fact that the absence of positive action to maintain the education in French in the municipalities in which they lived obliged the applicants either to enrol their children in the local Flemish schools or to send their children elsewhere, a cause of hardship and expense.

The Court considered that the facts complained of did not involve either a violation of Article 2 or a violation of Article 8 of the Convention itself, which is concerned with the protection of private and family life. The reasoning of the decision rested upon the premiss that the legislative history of the Convention did not support the view that positive action was necessary on the part of the State to provide subsidies and other material underpinning to the rights protected. In particular the Court observed:

> The legal provisions in issue, moreover, do not violate Article 8 of the Convention. It is true that one result of the Acts of 1932 and 1963 has been the disappearance in the Dutch unilingual region of the majority of schools providing education in French. Consequently French-speaking children living in this region can now obtain there only education in Dutch, unless their parents have the financial resources to send them to private French-language schools. This clearly has a certain impact upon family life when parents do not have sufficient means to enrol their children in a private school, or prefer that their children should avoid the inconvenience which the application of the law entails as regards education received in a private school which is not in conformity with the linguistic requirements of the laws on education. Such children will complete their studies in Dutch in the locality, unless their parents send them to school in Brussels, Wallonia, or abroad.
>
> Harsh though such consequences may be in individual cases, they do not involve any breach of Article 8. This provision in no way guarantees the right to be educated in

the language of one's parents by the public authorities or with their aid. Furthermore, in so far as the legislation leads certain parents to separate themselves from their children such a separation is not imposed by this legislation: it results from the choice of the parents who place their children in schools situated outside the Dutch unilingual region with the sole purpose of avoiding their being taught in Dutch, that is to say in one of Belgium's national languages.[8]

In the result the European Court did not favour positive action.

So that is the first special aspect of group rights, the claim to positive action. It is not suggested that the problem of positive action is only associated with the rights of groups, but the claim is more likely to be made in this context.

The second type of claim involving group rights is the claim to have adequate protection of land rights in traditional territories. The view that in certain societies there is a special connection between the people and the lands and waters of a region was articulated in the course of the Mackenzie Valley Pipeline Inquiry by the communities affected, and accepted by the Report compiled by the Commissioner, Mr Justice Thomas R. Berger, and published in 1977.[9] That is not, of course, the end of the matter, since the land rights question may, and usually does, involve issues of title, historic justice, and restitution. The central point, however, is the claim of rights directly related to exclusive rights in respect of specific areas. This sets the land rights issue, and the concept of traditional ownership of a group, apart from the usual prescription of human rights on the basis of individual protection.

The third type of claim specific to groups is based upon the political and legal principle of self-determination,

[8] Ser. A, no. 6, p. 43; 45 ILR 173–4.

[9] *Northern Frontier: Northern Homeland. The Report of the Mackenzie River Pipeline Inquiry*, 2 vols. (Ottawa, 1977), Mr Justice Thomas R. Berger.

the exercise of which involves a range of political models, including the choice of independent statehood or some form of autonomy or associated statehood. In practical terms, the recognition of group rights usually takes two forms. In the first place, there is the prescription of a basic standard of equality or non-discrimination. The general standard of non-discrimination is prescribed in both the International Covenant on Economic, Social, and Cultural Rights and the Covenant on Civil and Political Rights of 1966. The issue of racial discrimination is dealt with more comprehensively in the International Convention on the Elimination of All Forms of Racial Discrimination of 1965. New Zealand is a party to all three instruments.

The second form which recognition of group rights takes is the guarantee of the maintenance of group identity. As we have seen, Article 27 of the International Covenant on Civil and Political Rights provides that; 'In those States in which ethnic, religious or linguistic minorities exist, persons belonging to such minorities shall not be denied the right, in community with the other members of the group, to enjoy their own culture, to profess and practise their own religion, or to use their own language.' In the case of the protection of group rights, precisely because a very delicate balance of interests is called for, the existence of an efficient and sensitive legal system is immensely important. When the problems themselves are approached they are seen to be in many cases essentially difficult. The legal preservation, especially by positive action, of cultural identity may run the risk of appearing to erect principles of discrimination and the problem then becomes, when is discrimination tolerable on grounds of special need? The practical difficulties involved may be illustrated by two recent episodes, the first from Canada, the second from South Australia.

The first took the form of a decision by the Human

Rights Committee which has supervisory powers in respect of the International Covenant on Civil and Political Rights in accordance with the Optional Protocol to that Covenant. Canada, like New Zealand, is a party to the Optional Protocol. The decision resulted from a communication from a Canadian Indian which put in issue the interpretation of Article 27 of the covenant.[10] Sandra Lovelace, a registered Maliseet Indian, lost her status as an Indian under the Indian Act 1970 (Canada) when she married a non-Indian. An Indian man who married a non-Indian woman would not have lost his status in this way. Subsequently, her marriage broke up and she returned to live on the Reserve, contrary to the Act. She was only saved from eviction from the Reserve by threats made on her behalf against anyone attempting to remove her. She claimed violation of her rights under Article 2 of the Convention (on the basis that the Indian Act prevented her from enjoying her own culture in common with other members of the tribe). The Human Rights Committee took the view that, at least after she ceased to live with her husband and returned to the Reserve, the provisions of the Indian Act violated Article 27.

A recent Australian Law Reform Commission Research Paper[11] has this to say about Article 27:

> It is clear that one effect of Article 27 is to oblige a State to allow someone who is in fact a member of an ethnic minority group to associate with that group, even on reserve land, and that to this extent it imposes affirmative obligations. At least, legal impediments must not be placed in the way of the exercise of rights under Article 27, unless these have a 'reasonable and objective justification and [are] consistent with the other provisions of the Covenant'. It is also arguable

[10] Views of the Human Rights Committee under Art. 5 (4) of the Optional Protocol Concerning Communication, no. R6/24, 30 July 1981; *Report of the Human Rights Committee*, GAOR 36th Sess., Supp. no. 40 (A/36/40), Annex XVIII, 166; 68 ILR 17.

[11] *Research Paper No. 10* (prepared by J. R. Crawford), Nov. 1982, p. 15.

that the *failure* to make equivalent legal provision for members of minority groups could contravene Article 27 in particular cases, although it may be doubtful to what extent Article 27 imposes obligations on States to provide resources as distinct from legal rights or faculties.

The second episode, from South Australia, illustrates the way in which protective Land Rights legislation may be in danger of falling foul of human rights obligations arising under major international conventions, *at least as these are interpreted by the Australian courts*. The case concerned is *Gerhardy* v. *Brown*[12] decided by the High Court of Australia in 1985. The issue was the meaning of discrimination under the Commonwealth Racial Discrimination Act of 1975, which implements the International Convention on the Elimination of All Forms of Racial Discrimination of 1966. The key provision of the Act, section 8 (1), provides as follows:

> This Part does not apply to, or in relation to the application of, special measures to which paragraph 4 of Article 1 of the Convention applies except measures in relation to which subsection 10 (1) applies by virtue of sub-section 10 (3).

By Article 1, para. 4 of the Convention it is provided:

> 4. Special measures taken for the sole purpose of securing adequate advancement of certain racial or ethnic groups or individuals requiring such protection as may be necessary in order to ensure such groups or individuals equal enjoyment or exercise of human rights and fundamental freedoms shall not be deemed racial discrimination, provided, however, that such measures do not, as a consequence, lead to the maintenance of separate rights for different racial groups and that they shall not be continued after the objectives for which they were taken have been achieved.

[12] (1985) 159 CLR 70; 57 ALR 472.

The issue was whether the access to land provisions of the Pitjantjatjara Land Rights Act 1978 (SA) were racially discriminatory under the Commonwealth Act and the Convention. Their effect was to prevent any person other than a Pitjantjatjara (or a police officer, etc. in the course of official duties) entering the Pitjantjatjara land in the north-west of South Australia without a permit from the corporate body of the Pitjantjatjara. Brown, the defendant in the case, was in fact himself an aborigine, though not a Pitjantjatjara. The High Court held unanimously that there was no conflict between the South Australian provisions and the Commonwealth Act, on the ground that the South Australian Act (including its permit provisions) was a 'special measure' within the meaning of Article 1 (4) of the Convention, and section 8 (1) of the Act. However, six of the seven judges (Dawson J. not deciding) held that, in the absence of Article 1, para. 4, the provisions would have been discriminatory, because they made a distinction between Pitjantjatjara and non-Pitjantjatjara, one element of which was the proposition that to be a Pitjantjatjara was to be a member of a race. All the judges rejected the argument that the Act merely recognized traditional ownership and gave it effect within the general legal system, and that it was therefore not a discrimination based on race but a reasonable response to a traditional nexus to land. Accordingly, they treated Article 1, para. 1, of the Racial Discrimination Convention as implemented by sections 9 and 10 of the Act as being very much a prohibition on any formal discrimination by reference to a criterion containing any element of race irrespective of its 'legitimacy'. It follows that any provision containing notions of aboriginality will be prima facie discriminatory unless it can be saved under Article 1, para. 4.

The issues raised by *Gerhardy* v. *Brown* are familiar to the international lawyer and the international law materials have a particular value. No doubt the problems are to be examined very much in terms of their own time and social setting. However, the international experience indicates certain points of general technique. The most important point is that the fact that a primary criterion involves a reference to race does not make the rule discriminatory in law, provided the reference to race has an objective basis and a reasonable cause. It is only when the reference to race lacks a reasonable cause and is arbitrary that the rule concerned becomes discriminatory in the legal sense. Some examples can be given. Suppose that in a particular country, in an area of mixed population, special arrangements were made in State hospitals, prisons and so forth, to meet the particular dietary requirements of a racial or religious group. Two criteria would be relevant here: the membership of the racial or religious group and the dietary requirements. Again, in the context of sexual discrimination, it is obviously not discriminatory to make arrangements which are necessary to make allowance for the needs of women who are pregnant. The reference to the sex of the subject of the special provision is coupled with the second criterion, which is pregnancy.

Thus the question of discrimination is that of the *relevance* of the reference to race, or religion, or sex. Only women can become pregnant, but that does not mean that making special arrangements for pregnant women is in legal terms discrimination on grounds of sex. In the case of the recognition of the traditional ownership rights of the Pitjantjatjara the reference is similarly to a double criterion: that of tribal origin and that of traditional ownership. The fact that traditional ownership is peculiar to aborigines does not make recognition of such land rights discriminatory *in law*. The legal recognition has an objective basis; it is not arbitrary and is discriminatory only in the sense that a reasonable and legitimate policy *coincides* with racial origin, in the same way as pregnancy coincides with womanhood. Thus the first principle to apply is to ask whether the differentiation in the legal sense has a reasonable cause and relates to a legally relevant basis for different treatment.

The second principle is that the modalities of the different treatment must not be disproportionate in effect or involve unfairness to other racial groups. This is very much a factual issue, but the facts must themselves reflect some delicate nuances as to what is in local terms reasonable. In the case of the recognition of land rights, the restriction on freedom of movement, linked with such recognition, raises the issue of proportionality. In other words, even when the different treatment is not discriminatory in a legal sense, the modalities, the methods of implementation, may be unreasonable and hence discriminatory at the second level.

It is in the context of the principle of proportionality that the concept of affirmative action or reverse discrimination is to be seen. When a law prescribes for affirmative action, in effect the principle of proportionality is being explicitly set aside and normally this will only be done on carefully defined terms, one of which will be a time limit or other condition subsequently placed on the measures concerned. Article 1, para. 4 of the Convention on Racial Discrimination provides a justification for 'special measures' and stipulates that such measures 'shall not be continued after the objectives for which they were taken have been achieved'. It was this clause in the Convention, as reflected in the Act of 1975, which was the basis of the reasoning of the High Court in *Gerhardy* v. *Brown*. The difficulty is that the Hight Court appears to treat the 'special measures' clause as legitimating what would otherwise be discriminatory in law, since they view the legislation without that clause as being discriminatory. This approach is a further development of the original faulty premiss, which is the assumption by the High Court that the protection of traditional land rights is discriminatory in the first place.

There are many reasons, both legal and non-legal, for not conducting the inquiry in terms of the category of discrimination but rather in terms of the reasonableness of the objectives, the proportionality of the means employed, and the question of whether a special measure involves unfairness as between one group and another. The term 'discrimination' should only be applicable when the measure either favours or discriminates against a racial group without reasonable cause.

The approach through group rights in the context of international human rights standards provides one legal model for the resolution of questions of intercommunal equity in New Zealand. It is a reasonably helpful model, especially when it is undestood to include reference to the standards of international law in the sphere of human rights. The model also offers flexibility and is compatible with the existing legal and constitutional framework.

A further significant virtue consists in the fact that the human rights/group rights approach avoids the invidious concept of the 'protection of minorities'. The concept of minorities was essentially a by-product of the principle of national self-determination as applied in the continent of Europe. The concept of the minority was politically unpleasant and invited the view that members of minorities, the object of a special status, were quasi-aliens and of dubious allegiance. Moreover, the status of the minorities was the subject of international guarantees in the form of special treaties. In the relevant period (1920–39) there were very few *general* human rights standards and, as a result, the minority regimes were regarded as conferring privileges upon the minorities and as a discrimination against the

States on which they were imposed as a consequence of defeat or other accidents of politics. The League of Nations Covenant contained no general provisions constituting human rights standards. In any case, the minority protection model is irrelevant to the affairs of New Zealand, and would be a highly inappropriate mode of describing the status of the people who were the early arrivals in this country.

I must turn now to another well-known model for the recognition of group rights, that of self-determination. It is a principle generally recognized today,[13] although there is a certain hypocrisy about its application. In the western world the proponents of self-determination tend to envisage its application outside their own countries or regions. Similarly, Soviet exponents of self-determination have tended to propose its application to the colonial territories of European States and to Puerto Rico.

Historically, the principle of self-determination was a successor to the principle of nationalities which appeared in late eighteenth-century Europe. Its first targets were the Austro-Hungarian and Turkish Empires, and the Europe which emerged from the peace treaties of 1919 and 1920 reflected the principle to a great extent. During the drafting of the United Nations Charter express recognition was given to the principle, although for a considerable period after 1945 the colonial powers denied that it had become a part of international law. In my opinion it *has* done so, but its precise modalities, the methods of putting it into operation, are still being worked out.

The beneficiary of the right of self-determination may be described as a unit of self-determination, or in more ordinary language, a people or community with a distinct identity. There is continuing difficulty over the

[13] See I. Brownlie, *Principles of Public International Law*, 4th edn. (Oxford, 1990), 595–8.

definition of a 'people' for this purpose, and yet the concept has a core of reasonable certainty, which consists of the right of a community which has a distinct character to have this character reflected in the institutions of government under which it lives.[14] The concept of 'distinct character' depends on a number of criteria which may appear in varying combinations. Race is one of the relevant criteria but the concept of race is notoriously fugitive and in practical contexts it can only be expressed in terms of more specific elements, namely, culture, language, and group psychology. Moreover, there is no assumption that a unit of self-determination has to be racially homogeneous. Thus Canada, with or without Quebec, is racially very diverse but represents a good example of a composite unit of self-determination, the choice of a federal union being the form which has been taken in that case. The exercise of self-determination involves a wide range of political choices, including independent statehood, federal union, and various forms of autonomy or associated statehood.

In practice the question of the definition of a unit of self-determination is resolved by the process of recognition. There is here an analogy with the recognition of statehood in international law. Whilst it is not necessarily constitutive, recognition of a new State by pre-existing States produces very significant evidence of legal entitlement to statehood. Such recognition may take the form of a pattern of individual acts of recognition by other States or of a resolution of the General Assembly of the United Nations, or of a

[14] Cf. Tony Honoré, 'The Right to Rebel' (1988) 8 *OJLS* 34, cited in the Aotearoa–New Zealand context by F. M. Brookfield, 'Maori Rights and Two Radical Writers' [1990] *NZLJ* 406 at 416–17. Areas of Maori autonomy did in fact continue to exist long after the wars of the 1860s and early 1870s, perhaps not ending completely until the present century. See J. Belich, *The New Zealand Wars and the Victorian Interpretation of Racial Conflict* (Auckland, 1986), 302–10; K. Sinclair, *Kinds of Peace: Maori People after the Wars 1870—1885* (Auckland, 1991), 24–5, also Ch. 3.

regional organization, such resolutions being essentially collective acts of recognition. The Palestinians have been recognized as a people in a long series of UNGA resolutions. On occasion the procedure of self-determination involves a treaty: thus Cyprus gained independence in 1960 on the basis of a Treaty of Guarantee concluded by Cyprus of the one part, and Greece, Turkey, and the United Kingdom, of the other part.

How, if at all, do these concepts apply to the affairs of New Zealand? On the face of things, the Treaty of Waitangi could be represented as a form of self-determination on the part of the lawful representatives of the Maori people. In the modern context New Zealand is recognized as a State in international society, and the legitimacy of its government is not challenged on the international plane on the basis that its human rights performance is inadequate. For purposes of international law, New Zealand as such *is* a unit of self-determination. But even so, there is the possibility that the Maori people have a claim to self-determination or, more precisely, a *capacity* for self-determination, which they may exercise by opting for the *status quo* or otherwise.

Two difficulties confront the proposition that the Maori constitute a unit of self-determination. In the first place, the principle of self-determination is normally assumed to apply to a people in relation to a particular area of land, and not to a group interspersed with other groups. Thus the people of Afro-Caribbean origin living in the United Kingdom, or the Jewish population of France, may have certain group rights within the context of human rights standards, but it is doubtful whether they have a right to self-determination. It might be otherwise if the Maori were the dominant group of residents in a particular region, like the Dene or Indians of the North-West Territories of Canada.[15]

[15] See previous n.

There is, of course, the argument that the Maori, as the first people to arrive, cannot be discounted on this basis. It is doubtful if this argument is recognized in law, but in any case there is a second obstacle to the claim to be a unit of self-determination, and this is the Treaty of Waitangi itself. The provisions of the treaty actually take the form of a licence for British settlement, albeit on certain conditions. The society envisaged by the Treaty was essentially a plural society. Moreover, the alienation of land was expressly permitted without any restriction *on a regional basis.* There were to be no reserved areas, although section 71 of the Constitution Act of 1852[16] envisaged the creation of special districts with cultural autonomy.

However, even if it is difficult to establish that the Maori people constitute a unit of self-determination, certain important questions are not precluded and remain to be resolved. For, after all, the cession effected by the Treaty of Waitangi was accompanied by important conditions. If reference is made to Lord Normanby's instructions to Captain Hobson, it can readily be appreciated that land alienation was not intended to impinge upon the fundamental rights of the Maori, as is evident from the last paragraph of the previously quoted passage:

[16] The section, which was never given effect, read: 'And whereas it may be expedient that the laws, customs, and usages of the aboriginal or [Maori] inhabitants of New Zealand, so far as they are not repugnant to the general principles of humanity, should for the present be maintained for the government of themselves, in all their relations to and dealings with each other, and that particular districts should be set apart within which such laws, customs, or usages should be so observed: It shall be lawful for Her Majesty, by any letters patent to be issued under the Great Seal of the United Kingdom, from time to time to make provision for the purposes aforesaid, any repugnancy of any such [Maori] laws, customs, or usages to the law of England, or to any law, statute, or usage in force in New Zealand, or in any part thereof, in anywise notwithstanding.' As to Maori requests that the section be given effect, see Orange, *Treaty*, 212, 215, 222. Section 71 was retained in the Act of 1852 until the latter was repealed (in New Zealand law) by the Constitution Act 1986 (see Ch. 1, n. 17), in which there is no corresponding provision.

> All dealings with the Aborigines for their Lands must be conducted on the same principles of sincerity, justice, and good faith as must govern your transactions with them for the recognition of Her Majesty's Sovereignty in the Islands. Nor is this all. They must not be permitted to enter into any Contracts in which they might be the ignorant and unintentional authors of injuries to themselves. You will not, for example, purchase from them any Territory the retention of which by them would be essential, or highly conducive, to their own comfort, safety or subsistence. The acquisition of Land by the Crown for the future Settlement of British Subjects must be confined to such Districts as the Natives can alienate without distress or serious inconvenience to themselves. To secure the observance of this rule will be one of the first duties of their official protector.[17]

The brutal fact is that the Treaty of Waitangi has been and remains a very inefficient vehicle of this intention to balance interests.

The question of equity between early and subsequent arrivals depends on the following agenda in so far as land titles are concerned:

1. The review of irregular dispositions to the prejudice of Maori groups or individuals.
2. The restoration of marae and other sites of special significance even in the absence of evidence of irregular dispositions.
3. The restoration of titles to other lands and resources (for example, fisheries) where the Crown can show no countervailing interest of the community as a whole, and the object is an equitable redistribution.

In this context, the Treaty of Waitangi Act is of importance, not simply because it provides machinery for restitution and its proxies, but because it is based upon a broad and flexible concept of interests which are, or are likely to be, 'prejudicially affected'. Furthermore, it is very likely that the international conventions

[17] See n. 5 above.

to which New Zealand is a party provide a source of instruments for the fashioning of a regime of restitution which allows for a balancing up of the interests of all the communities living in New Zealand. The general principles of equality and proportionality will also be highly relevant.

The Treaty of Waitangi and the Act of 1975 both address the land question. There are several questions they do not address, and the general issue of gaps in the system is dealt with in my final lecture. However, there is one gap in the system which should receive attention at this stage. It is this: if the Maori were to be recognized as a unit of self-determination, or to be in an analogous position, they would have certain claims to protection analogous to those which a State has to protect its independence and territorial integrity.

It is perfectly reasonable to apply the concepts of integrity and authenticity to a unit of self-determination. In some regions of the world the sinister weapon of demographic manipulation is used to bring about substantial change in the demographic *status quo*. For years complaint has been made about Israeli settlements on a racial basis in the Occupied Territories, and similar complaints are made by the Government of Cyprus in relation to the settlement of people from Turkey in the occupied areas of Cyprus since the Turkish invasion of 1974. These examples involve demographic change as a deliberate instrument of national policy, and such cases are often associated with the use of force and military occupation. The situation of New Zealand is very different and there is, in any case, a certain doubt as to whether Maori have the right to self-determination.

This notwithstanding, they can reasonably claim to have a legitimate interest in the ethnic composition and population densities in the country as a whole, the basis for which would consist of the Treaty of Waitangi and the Instructions of Lord Normanby to Captain Hobson. Both instruments make it fairly clear that the bargain did not involve settlement from outside without any limitations. There can be no doubt that the question of equity as between early arrivals and late arrivals cannot leave out of account the issue of immigration and the control of population densities.

It will be helpful at this point to produce a brief balance-sheet of the approach to intercommunal equity on the basis of group rights as an aspect of human rights standards. This approach has much to offer. The instruments would then include the international conventions to which New Zealand is a party, provided they were incorporated into New Zealand law by appropriate legislation, and the principles of general international law concerning human rights.

On the other hand, the concept of self-determination in its classical mode appears not to be relevant to the situation. However, as I have tried to point out, there are at least certain analogies with the principle of self-determination. In order to create and maintain an equitable basis for the relations of Maori and other communities it is necessary to implement principles and policies involving affirmative action. The justification for such policies is to be found in the Treaty of Waitangi and in the legislation of 1975 and 1985. The reliance on human rights standards will need to be supplemented by the concepts derived from group rights and from the analogies with self-determination.

The New Zealand situation lies uneasily between the ordinary human-rights model and the self-determination model. In legal terms it is a plural society qualified by a legal recognition of a set of criteria of intercommunal equity based on the Treaty and a programme of restitution also based on the Treaty. The rule of law in New Zealand tends to be based on the model of individual rights, whilst the programme of restitution and equitable adjustment is based in part upon the recognition of group rights.

There is, however, a further model for the recognition and protection of group rights, and that is the concept of indigenous peoples which will be dealt with in my third lecture.

3

Indigenous Peoples: A Relevant Concept?

IN the second lecture the various models based upon the concept of group rights were examined, including those of self-determination and the protection of minorities. The topic of indigenous peoples was reserved for this, the third lecture.

The Maori are by any criterion within the description of indigenous peoples. Moreover, the term 'indigenous' more or less proposes a criterion of antecedence. Thus the concept of indigenous peoples has a prominent place on the agenda. The task is to discover its relevance to the issue of equity as between Maori and Pakeha. The term 'indigenous' as a synonym for 'native', meaning one born in a particular land or region, is of ancient usage in Europe, where the terms employed in the early nineteenth century were 'native' or 'aboriginal'. In Lord Normanby's Instructions to Captain Hobson the terms used interchangeably are 'the Natives' and 'the Aborigines of New Zealand'. It is clear that the Maori are regarded as a group with an obvious identity. At the same time the actual party to the Treaty consisted of the chiefs of the Confederation and of the sub-tribes of New Zealand[1] as a corporate body, and thus the Treaty involved the Confederation as previously recognized in its capacity as an international person. In Lord Normanby's Instructions,[2]

[1] See Ch. 1, n. 9 and text.

[2] Quoted above in text at Ch. 2, n. 5.

New Zealand is referred to as 'a Sovereign and independent State', the sovereignty of which is described as 'indisputable'.

There is not much more to be said about the history of the term 'indigenous people'. Prior to the Second World War the term 'indigenous people' was not fashionable, except in the context of certain Conventions adopted by the ILO in the years 1930–9, which referred to 'indigenous workers'. Since 1945 the terminology has become much more common. In the first place, it has been regarded as an acceptable substitute for the term 'natives', which had become associated with concepts of hierarchy and discrimination.[3] Secondly, in the era of decolonization it was found useful to have a term for certain groups who remained vulnerable after decolonization had transferred power to the dominant group in the territory concerned. Without going into detail, it can be stated that the history suggests that vulnerability was a criterion at least as significant as antecedence.

Since 1945 the protection of indigenous peoples has been more prominently on the political agenda. Three strands of activity can be discerned. In the first place, the ILO has focused on the problem of indigenous workers as a result of stimulus from various Latin-American States. This work culminated in Conventions adopted in 1957 and 1989.[4] Secondly, the United Nations Human Rights Sub-Commission on Prevention of Discrimination and Protection of Minorities has taken up the question of indigenous people. The consequence was the appointment in 1972 of a Special Rapporteur on the problem of discrimination against

[3] In New Zealand official usage, 'Maori' replaced 'native' in accordance with Part I of the Maori Purposes Act 1947.

[4] In 1957 the International Labour Conference adopted Convention 107 on the Protection of Indigenous and other Tribal and Semi-Tribal Populations in Independent Countries, *UNTS* 328, pp. 247–69. In June 1989, after four years of preparatory work, the International Labour Conference adopted a revised version of Convention 107 (Convention 169).

indigenous populations, José Martinez Cobo, who presented a final report in 1983.[5] In 1982 the Sub-Commission established a Working Group on Indigenous Populations. In addition, in 1985 the United Nations General Assembly set up the United Nations Fund for Indigenous Populations to assist representatives of indigenous organizations and communities to participate in the activities of the Working Group. It is administered by the Secretary-General on the basis of recommendations made by a Board of Trustees. At the 1989 session of the Working Group in Geneva, indigenous peoples were represented by delegations from Argentina, Australia, Bolivia, Brazil, Chile, Colombia, Costa Rica, Ecuador, Guatemala, India, Mexico, New Zealand, Nicaragua, Panama, Paraguay, Peru, Philippines, Surinam, Tanzania, the United States, and Venezuela.

The present schedule of the Working Group on Indigenous Populations focuses upon the preparation of a draft Universal Declaration on the Rights of Indigenous Peoples. Ms Erica-Irene Daes, the Chairman-Rapporteur of the Working Group, submitted a first revised text of the draft in 1989.[6] Work on a second revised text is now proceeding. As a part of this process the New Zealand Government has established a process of consultation with the tangata whenua.[7]

[5] The full report was issued in consolidated form as UN Doc. E/CN. 4/ Sub. 2/ 1986/7/Add. 1–4, with the title, 'Study of the Problem of Discrimination against Indigenous Populations'.

[6] See the New Zealand official publication: *Declaration on the Rights of Indigenous Peoples: Consultation with the Tangata Whenua*, Ministry of External Affairs and Trade, no date.

[7] See the previous note; and cf. *Legislative Change: Guidelines on Process and Content*, Report by the Legislation Advisory Committee, revd. edn. (1991), para. 41. A general duty for the Crown to consult with Maori (about governmental matters affecting them) in pursuance of the Treaty, in the context of a statute requiring the Crown to act in accordance with the 'principles' of the Treaty, was not recognized by the Court of Appeal in *New Zealand Maori Council* v. *Attorney-General* [1987] 1 NZLR 641. See at 665 (Cooke P.), 682–3 (Richardson J.), 693 (Somers J.). But a duty to consult on 'truly major issues' was recognized by that Court in *New Zealand Maori Council* v. *Attorney-General* [1989] 2 NZLR 142 at 152.

The third strand of activity has been the non-governmental organizations. The inaugural meeting of the World Council of Indigenous Peoples was held in Canada in 1975 and was attended by a representative of the Maori Council. The other relevant non-governmental organizations are the Four Directions Council, the Indigenous World Association, the International Indian Treaty Council, the Indian Law Resource Centre, the Indian Council of South America, the Inuit Circumpolar Conference, the National Aboriginal and Islander Legal Service Secretariat, and the National Indian Youth Council.[8]

That, then, is the historical background. The legal ramifications of indigeneity remain to be teased out. The lawyer must first call up a definition of the beneficiaries. At this point the non-lawyer grows impatient. Lawyers sometimes seem like the lady who did not know what an elephant was until she was told it was a herbivorous pachyderm. Moreover, in the case of indigenous peoples there is the feeling that the only acceptable procedure is that of self-identification. However, definition is not simply the satisfying of arid formalism but helps to round up certain difficult questions of purpose. In particular, the question of whether it is necessary to distinguish indigenous peoples from other ethnic groups. In this context the purpose, whatever it be, in identifying the beneficiaries of any special legal regime which may be required, must be to link the entitlements with the beneficiaries. If the regime involves a *reciprocal* relationship between an indigenous people *and other groups within the State,* it becomes necessary to have an objective definition of the groups involved, because otherwise it is difficult to envisage a stable and equitable legal regime.

[8] See *The Rights of Indigenous Peoples,* UN Centre for Human Rights, Geneva, Fact Sheet No. 9 (1990), 3–4.

To move the discussion forward, it is helpful to present two exemplary definitions. The first is the tentative definition proposed by the Special Rapporteur of the Sub-Commission of the UN Human Rights Commission, Mr José Martinez Cobo. The text is as follows:

> Indigenous communities, peoples and nations are those which, having a historical continuity with pre-invasion and pre-colonial societies that developed on their territories, consider themselves distinct from other sectors of the societies now prevailing in those territories, or parts of them. They form at present non-dominant sectors of society and are determined to preserve, develop and transmit to future generations their ancestral territories, and their ethnic identity, as the basis of their continued existence as peoples, in accordance with their own cultural patterns, social institutions and legal systems.
>
> This historical continuity may consist of the continuation, for an extended period reaching into the present, of one or more of the following factors:
>
> (*a*) Occupation of ancestral lands, or at least of part of them;
> (*b*) Common ancestry with the original occupants of these lands;
> (*c*) Culture in general, or in specific manifestations (such as religion, living under a tribal system, membership of an indigenous community, dress, means of livelihood, life-style, etc.);
> (*d*) Language (whether used as the only language, as mother-tongue, as the habitual means of communication at home or in the family, or as the main, preferred, habitual general or normal language);
> (*e*) Residence in certain parts of the country, or in certain regions of the world;
> (*f*) Other relevant factors.[9]

[9] E/CN. 4/Sub. 2/1986/7/Add. 4, paras. 378–80.

Whatever faults this definition may have, it has been adopted by the Working Group for practical purposes, but no definitive formulation has been established.

There are three comments to be made. First, the approach places much emphasis on antecedence, and the general result is that, apart from the factor of priority of settlement, there is little or nothing to distinguish an indigenous people from any other ethnic group. Secondly, a particular characteristic of certain types of traditional aboriginal culture is its vulnerability in the face of economic individualism and entrepreneurial pressures. Hence the legal regime adopted in Australia to preserve the life-style of aboriginal tribes still in possession of ancestral lands. Yet the Martinez Cobo definition makes no reference to the factor of vulnerability.

Thirdly, this definition, as applied in United Nations' practice, has laid emphasis on the criterion that indigenous peoples form non-dominant sectors of society. This criterion of non-dominance is not very apt, as it is not a necessary condition of indigenous peoples. In any event, a more signfiicant criticism is that the issue is not dominance but equality, and equality within the principles and standards of the law concerning human rights. The emphasis on dominance/non-dominance is unhelpful and inimical to the application of legal principles to establish equity.

The definition employed in the ILO Convention on indigenous populations adopted in 1989, employs two sets of criteria to identify the groups to which the Convention applies. Article 1 (1) of Convention 169 provides that the convention applies to:

(*a*) tribal peoples in independent countries whose social, cultural and economic conditions distinguish them from other sections of the national community, and whose status is regulated wholly or partially by their own customs or traditions or by special laws or regulations;

(*b*) peoples in independent countries who are regarded as indigenous on account of their descent from the populations which inhabited the country, or a geographical region to which the country belongs, at the time of conquest or colonisation or the establishment of present State boundaries and who, irrespective of their legal status, retain some or all of their own social, economic, cultural and political institutions.

It is obvious that these definitions are not easy to apply, and there are marked differences in the practice of States. The reference to 'tribal peoples' is difficult to apply in practice. However, it is the second classification which has greater complexities, as it presents three criteria which are only sufficient in combination. The criteria are

1. descent from certain groups;
2. antecedence of these groups compared with others; and
3. retention of separate institutions (in whole or in part).

These cumulative criteria tend to be exclusive in effect. Moreover, the criterion of antecedence may be controversial and the Government of India has refused to accept that the so-called Scheduled Tribes and other tribal groups are 'indigenous peoples' because it is impossible as a matter of fact to establish which groups were antecedent. The Chinese Government has the same approach.

The difficulties of definition having been pursued so as to shed some light on the nature of the concept, it is important now to examine the legal ramifications of the classification of 'indigenous peoples'. It has to be said at the outset that general or customary international law does not present any rules or principles concerning indigenous peoples *as such*. But this is far from saying that general international law has no relevance to the affairs of indigenous peoples. The fact is that the general stock of human rights standards, including the principle of non-discrimination and the concept of group rights, applies to the affairs of indigenous peoples. This follows as a matter of general principle, but it is also borne out by the case-load of such institutions as the UN Human Rights Committee related to the Civil and Political Rights Covenant, and the Inter-American Commission of Human Rights. In particular, Article 27 of the International Covenant on Civil and Political Rights is relevant and its provisions were applied in the *Sandra Lovelace* case before the Human Rights Committee.[10] In the same way, the International Convention on the Elimination of All Forms of Racial Discrimination provides protection for the rights of indigenous peoples.

There can be little doubt that the normal application of human rights standards should take care of most of the legitimate concerns of indigenous peoples and, if this is correct, then the continuing controversy over the definition of indigenous peoples is not of great significance, apart from the application of certain ILO Conventions tied to the identification of either 'tribal' peoples or 'indigenous' peoples. There is, however, more to be said about the status of indigenous peoples in general international law. The majority of States have been reluctant to accept legal obligations specifically based upon the categorization. The significance of this reluctance is difficult to quantify. States are already bound by norms of general international law to respect the human rights of racial or religious groups, so they are not avoiding responsibility in this respect. Moreover, the principle of self-determination is applicable to the

[10] See Ch. 2, n. 10.

affairs of distinctive groups on certain conditions, and these conditions do not make a capacity for self-determination depend on satisfying criteria of tribalism or indigeneity. Many writers—scholars, as the Americans like to say—are specialists in human rights, rather than general international law, and specialists in indigenous peoples rather than human rights. Some, at least, of these super-specialists suffer from super tunnel vision. It does not seem to occur to them that their subject of special interest belongs to a much wider world of normative development and, what is more, a world in which the concepts lying to hand have more fluency and political acceptability.

The heavy reliance on the still relatively controversial category of 'indigenous peoples' is difficult to understand and, frankly, it smacks of nominalism and a sort of snobbery. There is at the moment a well-organized public relations effort being conducted on behalf of the Tibetan people. Their life style is by any standards traditional but the Tibetan exile leadership is not relying on the concept of indigenous peoples, but on the principles of human rights and self-determination.

In spite of the absence of norms of general international law expressly designed to protect the interests of indigenous peoples, there are two general multilateral treaties dealing specifically with their position. The first of these is ILO Convention 107. It is entitled 'Convention No. 107 concerning the Protection and Integration of Indigenous and other Tribal and Semi-Tribal Populations in Independent Countries', and was concluded on 26 June 1957.[11] The Convention has been ratified by at least twenty-seven States, but has not been ratified by the United States, Canada, the USSR, or New Zealand. The substance of the Convention has received mixed reviews. Its general purpose, reflected

[11] See n. 4 above.

in its title, was to assist integration, and such assimilationist policies are now regarded with reserve. Indeed, the Australian Government has explained its decision not to ratify the Convention in the following terms:

> the Government had had under further examination the thrust of the provisions of the Convention. It considers that there are a number of outmoded concepts in Convention No. 107. The Convention's emphasis on 'integration' does not for example accord with the Government's policy of recognizing the fundamental right of Aboriginals to retain their identity and traditional life style where desired. We understand that the ILO is looking at the possible need to redefine the objectives of the Convention, replacing the present emphasis on integration by the principle of respect for the indigenous population's identity and wishes.
>
> As things stand, the Government feels that there are other international Conventions to which Australia is already a party, viz. the Convention on the Elimination of All Forms of Racial Discrimination, and the Covenants on Civil and Political Rights and on Economic, Social and Cultural Rights, which better serve the interests of Australian Aboriginals.[12]

The general flavour of Convention 107 can be discerned by reference to the provisions of Articles 3 and 4, as follows:

Article 3

1. So long as the social, economic and cultural conditions of the populations concerned prevent them from enjoying the benefits of the general laws of the country to which they belong, special measures shall be adopted for the protection of the institutions, persons, property and labour of these populations.
2. Care shall be taken to ensure that such special measures of protection—
   (*a*) are not used as a means of creating or prolonging a state of segregation; and

[12] Sen. Chaney, Senate, 25 Aug. 1982; Commonwealth Parliament, *Daily Hansard* (Senate), 25 Aug. 1982, 517 (quoted in *Research Paper No. 10*, Australian Law Reform Commission, Nov. 1982, p. 10).

(*b*) will be continued only so long as there is need for special protection and only to the extent that such protection is necessary.

3. Enjoyment of the general rights of citizenship, without discrimination, shall not be prejudiced in any way by such special measures of protection.

Article 4

In applying the provisions of this Convention relating to the integration of the populations concerned—

(*a*) due account shall be taken of the cultural and religious values and of the forms of social control existing among these populations, and of the nature of the problems which face them both as groups and as individuals when they undergo social and economic change;

(*b*) the danger involved in disrupting the values and institutions of the said populations unless they can be replaced by appropriate substitutes which the groups concerned are willing to accept shall be recognised;

(*c*) policies aimed at mitigating the difficulties experienced by these populations in adjusting themselves to new conditions of life and work shall be adopted.

The second general multilateral convention is ILO Convention 169, which was adopted in 1989 and constitutes a revision of the previous Convention.[13] The parties to the Convention (when it enters into force) will be responsible, with the participation of the peoples concerned, for developing action to protect the rights of these peoples, and to guarantee respect for their integrity. Duties are prescribed in relation to the protection of their persons, institutions, cultures, and environment. In applying the Convention, Governments shall in good faith consult the peoples concerned whenever consideration is being given to measures which may affect them directly, and establish means for their participation in decision-making elective institutions and other bodies. The peoples concerned have the

[13] See n. 4 above.

right to decide their own development priorities and Governments have the duty to protect the environment of the territories they inhabit.

The Convention also provides for the recognition of rights of ownership and possession of indigenous peoples over lands which they traditionally occupy. Their rights to natural resources pertaining to the lands they occupy are to be safeguarded. And, finally, unlawful intrusion upon their lands is to be punished with adequate penalties.

The political organs of the United Nations have taken a certain interest in the question of indigenous peoples, but that interest has usually taken the form of incidental references contained in General Assembly resolutions relating to general issues of human rights or the situation of human rights in a given country. Thus General Assembly resolutions concerning such diverse topics as the Second Decade to Combat Racism and Racial Discrimination, the Report of the Committee on the Elimination of Racial Discrimination, the human rights situation in Chile, and the human rights situation in Guatemala, have all contained references to the well-being of indigenous populations.

Otherwise, the work of the United Nations has been exploratory but significant none the less. In this context the work of the Sub-Commission of the United Nations Commission on Human Rights has been outstanding. One aspect of this work has been the commissioning of Ms Daes, as Chairman-Rapporteur of the Working Group, to produce a draft Universal Declaration on the Rights of Indigenous Peoples.[14] The fact remains that in the sphere of law-making activity and the sponsorship of legally binding instruments, the United Nations has not done anything substantial to recognize the interests

[14] See n. 6 above. See also the analytical commentary on the draft principles contained in the first revised text, E/CN. 4/Sub. 2/1990/39, 29 June 1990.

of indigenous peoples outside the agenda of normal human rights protection.

The task of the Working Group on Indigenous Populations is far from complete. The Group consists of five independent experts, currently from Greece, Yugoslavia, China, Cuba, and Nigeria. Their final draft must be acceptable to the General Assembly. Much will turn on the pattern of voting on the Declaration. In any event the present draft contains some controversial provisions. Thus paragraph 23 would recognize:

> The [collective] right to autonomy in matters relating to [indigenous peoples'] own internal and local affairs, including education, information, culture, religion, health, housing, social welfare, traditional and other economic activities, land and resources administration and the environment, as well as internal taxation for financing these autonomous functions.

The Organization of American States has, among the family of regional organizations, been the most frequently concerned with issues affecting indigenous peoples. In particular, the Organization convened eight Inter-American Indian Conferences in the period 1940–81.

Having set forth the experience hitherto, one must now relate all this to the situation in New Zealand, and to show to what extent the 'indigenous peoples' concept and the related developments offer benefits to Maori people. As a preliminary matter, it is worth pointing out that the legal politics of human and group rights does not consist of a zero sum game. Thus it appears perfectly possible to keep all options open and to retain legitimate claims to protection from normal human rights standards and/or the principle of self-determination, whilst relying, in part at least, on the special protection which may be afforded by the concept of indigenous peoples. The first benefit is the opportunity, in the work of the Sub-Commission at

Geneva and in various non-governmental organizations, to share experience with other groups having similar interests. In this way lobbying and publicity techniques are improved and morale maintained or improved. There can also be an exchange of experience in the use of legal methods of upholding rights or furthering changes in the *status quo*.

Another benefit is the likelihood that acceptance of the norms relating to indigenous peoples will provide a firmer base for the pursuit of legal goals in the sphere of affirmative action than the orthodox principles and standards of international law concerning human rights. This is particularly so with reference to the use of the law to attain the more radical goals of achieving intercommunal equity in relation to land ownership and access to natural resources.

There can be little doubt that the concept of the special status of indigenous peoples has particular relevance in the context of the right to possession of land traditionally occupied by the group. Even the often-criticized ILO Convention 107 adopted in 1957 contains the following provision in Article 11: 'The right of ownership, collective or individual, of the members of the populations concerned over the lands which these populations traditionally occupy shall be recognised.' Whilst this Article recognizes a principle, Article 12 indicates flexibility in its application, but provides for forms of compensation when people are removed from traditional lands:

1. The populations concerned shall not be removed without their free consent from their habitual territories except in accordance with national laws and regulations for reasons relating to national security, or in the interest of national economic development or of the health of the said populations.
2. When in such cases removal of these populations is necessary as an exceptional measure, they shall be

provided with lands of quality at least equal to that of the lands previously occupied by them, suitable to provide for their present needs and future development. In cases where chances of alternative employment exist and where the populations concerned prefer to have compensation in money or in kind, they shall be so compensated under appropriate guarantees.

3. Persons thus removed shall be fully compensated for any resulting loss or injury.

The Report commissioned by the Sub-Commission on the Prevention of Discrimination and the Protection of Minorities presented in 1983 by Mr Martinez Cobo, the Special Rapporteur, pays considerable attention to land rights. The principal recommendations on land rights are:

511. It must be recognized that indigenous peoples have a natural and inalienable right to retain the territories they possess, to call for the return of land of which they have been deprived and to be free to decide as to their use and development.

512. Genuine guarantees should be provided and full effect given to the right of indigenous populations to the land which they and their ancestors have worked since time immemorial and to the resources which such land contains, as well as to traditional forms of land tenure and resource exploitation.

514. Recognition must be given to the right of all indigenous nations or peoples, as a minimum, to the return and control of sufficient and suitable land to enable them to live an economically viable existence in accordance with their own customs and traditions, and to develop fully at their own pace . . .

516. Millenary or immemorial possession and economic occupation should suffice to establish indigenous title to land . . .

519. . . . Land occupied and controlled by indigenous populations should be presumed to be indigenous land. In case of doubt or dispute the *onus probandi* of

the ownership of land should fall . . . on the non-indigenous populations who claim to have acquired a right to part of the land.

520. All indigenous reserved areas should be immediately handed over to the respective indigenous groups . . .

521. Public land which is sacred or of religious significance to the indigenous populations should be attributed to them in perpetuity.

524. . . . No intermediary institution of any kind should be created or appointed to hold the lands of indigenous peoples on their behalf.

526. A protective regime should cover indigenous land . . . This regime should at least include restrictions on alienation, encumbrance, attachment and proscription . . .

528. All illegal acquisition of indigenous land should be null and void *ab initio* and no rights should be vested in subsequent purchasers or acquirers of the land . . .

532. Indigenous populations should be compensated for the loss of all . . . lands that have been or may be taken.

543. . . . the resources of the subsoil of indigenous land also must be regarded as the exclusive property of indigenous communities. Where this is rendered impossible by the fact that the deposits in the subsoil are the preserve of the State, the State must . . . allow full participation by indigenous communities in respect of:

— the granting of exploration and exploitation licences;

— the profits generated by such operations, and

— procedures for determining damage caused and compensation payable.[15]

Similar formulations appear in the draft Universal Declaration on the Rights of Indigenous Peoples.

[15] UN Doc. E/CN. 4/Sub. 2/1983/21/Add. 8 (and E/CN. 4/Sub. 2/1986/7/ Add. 4).

In the same vein a Preparatory Meeting of Indigenous Peoples convened in Geneva prior to the session of the Working Group on Indigenous Populations in 1987 adopted a Declaration of Principles[16] of which the fourth paragraph read: 'Indigenous nations and peoples are entitled to the permanent control and enjoyment of their aboriginal ancestral-historical territories. This includes air space, surface and subsurface rights, inland and coastal waters, sea ice, renewable and non-renewable resources, and the economies based on those resources.' There are also claims to be found in the literature that indigenous peoples as such are beneficiaries of the right to development. However, the General Assembly's Declaration on the Right to Development adopted in 1986[17] makes no reference to the position of indigenous peoples, and the general emphasis in the text is on the entitlements of individuals. At the same time, it is clear that indigenous peoples have a place *among* the beneficiaries of the right to development, and this was acknowledged by the Waitangi Tribunal in its *Report on the Muriwhenua Fishing Claim* in 1988.[18]

Thus far the concept of indigenous peoples has been taken as a datum, a part of legal development to be accepted without challenge, and the benefits which can be derived from it have been chronicled. All this has been done in a spirit of professional objectivity. This same spirit of professional objectivity leads to a further and complementary set of observations. The question of what is to be done will be examined from the Maori point of view, because the Maori people alone have the real choice of taking hold of the category of indigenous people. At one level it is obviously good tactics for the

[16] UN Doc. E/CN. 4/Sub. 2/1987/22, Annex V.

[17] Resol. 41/128, adopted on 4 Dec. 1986. See further Brownlie, *The Human Right to Development*, Commonwealth Secretariat, Human Rights Unit Occasional Paper, Nov. 1989.

[18] Wai-22 (1988), 234–5.

Maori people to maintain contact with the UN Sub-Commission's Working Group and the deliberations of the relevant non-governmental organizations, but whether it is good policy for Maori to attach themselves exclusively to the flag of the indigenous peoples, to accept this legal and political classification without reservation, should be questioned. In the first place, there is no mandatory principle according to which groups who qualify as indigenous peoples are indelibly characterized as such. Secondly, the world of indigenous peoples is extremely wide socially and politically, and one should be wary about a classification which is so comprehensive. Each people has its own history and culture, and to bracket the Maori with the Inuit, the Australian aboriginal, the Central American Indian, or the Solomon Islander (who is independent) may be logical, but only at a certain level of political abstraction.

Above all, the history of New Zealand is concrete and not abstract, and the Treaty of Waitangi and its legislative offshoots constitute a regime with its own particular characteristics. Acceptance of the Treaty of Waitangi and the principles deduced from it by the Waitangi Tribunal and the Courts creates obstacles to the adoption of a legal programme at odds with the Treaty. And adherence to an unmodified and monolithic indigenous people programme would constitute the polar opposite, legally speaking, of the position adopted by Chief Justice Prendergast in 1877.[19] Both his nullity approach and the view that the presence of Pakeha has only a relative legitimacy[20] are equally incompatible

[19] See *Wi Parata* v. *Bishop of Wellington* (1877) 3 NZ Jur. (NS) SC 72 at 78. Prendergast CJ, delivering his joint judgment with Richmond J., expressed the view that the Treaty was a 'simple nullity'.

[20] Legal writers whose work, either generally or on occasion, gives at least implied support to this view include notably D. V. Williams and J. Kelsey. See D. V. Williams in I. H. Kawharu (ed.), *Waitangi: Māori and Pākehā Perspectives of the Treaty of Waitangi* (Auckland, 1989), 64 and, for other of his writings, 'The Queen *v.* Symonds Reconsidered' (1989) 19 *VUWLR* 385, and 'The Constitutional Status of the Treaty of Waitangi . . .' (1990) 14 *NZULR* 9,

with the principles of Waitangi based upon common citizenship.

In any event, the adoption within New Zealand of a legal strategy based upon the concept of indigenous peoples would present some problems from a Maori point of view. My opinion is that the issues of intercommunal equity should be pursued within the general context of human rights principles and standards, and the relevant international conventions. In this way the concepts of partnership and racial equality based upon the Waitangi Treaty can be given content and application by reference to a wider set of legal norms and concepts.

Against this background, and from a strictly legal point of view, the approach based upon the concept of indigenous people has the considerable drawback that it represents a claim not of equality but of priority and privilege. It is one thing to obtain some advantages within a flexible application of equality and within a regime of restitution of land rights. It is quite another thing to operate categorically within a regime of privilege and exclusiveness. For the law leans against discrimination, and human rights standards require that the presumption is against discrimination, unless

and below. For Kelsey's work, see e.g. her *A Question of Honour? Labour and the Treaty 1984–1989* (Wellington, 1990); 'Legal Imperialism and the Colonization of Aotearoa' in P. Spoonley *et al.* (eds.), *Tauiwi: Racism and Ethnicity in New Zealand* (Palmerston North, 1984), 20–43; 'Decolonization in the "First World"' (1985) 5 *Windsor Yearbook of Access to Justice* 102; '"Rogernomics" and the Treaty of Waitangi . . .' (1989) 7 *Law in Context* 66; and 'The Treaty of Waitangi and Maori Independence . . .' (1990) *9th Commonwealth Law Conference Papers*, 249. See also *Te Whakamarama: The Maori Law Bulletin*, e.g. no. 8 (1991) (several writers), and the case and legislation analysis by A. L. Mikaere ('Maori Issues I') in [1989] *NZRL Rev.* 170, and [1990] *NZRLR* 122; as well as by Williams ('Maori Issues II') [1989] *NZRL Rev.* 177, and [1990] *NZRL Rev.* 129. Non-legal writing from radical viewpoints includes D. Awatere, *Maori Sovereignty* (Auckland, 1984); and essays by several of the contributors to H. Yensen *et al.* (eds.), *Honouring the Treaty* (Auckland, 1989), which also contains contributions by Williams and Kelsey. Some of the work of the two last-named is discussed by F. M. Brookfield [1990] *NZLJ* 406.

there are special circumstances. The burden of proof is therefore upon the proponent of discrimination.

There are yet other disadvantages in an exclusive adherence to the category of indigenous peoples. A somewhat neglected topic in the subject of human rights is the collision of one set of goals or values with some distinct set of goals or values. The more rigorous view of indigenous peoples involves what may be called the total preservation syndrome, which places traditional values above all else, including human rights norms and environmental programmes. On this strict view, if, for the sake of illustration, traditional or indigenous treatment of women falls short of contemporary human rights standards, then too bad for human rights standards. Other tensions can be envisaged, not necessarily relevant to New Zealand, in the context of traditional punishments or the cultural equivalent of expatriation, when individuals choose non-traditional life-styles or compromises. There is a strange tendency for some liberal non-indigenous people to favour extreme historicism in non-dominant groups which in dominant groups they would regard as abhorrent and verging on the feudal.

With this lecture I have finally completed my canvass of the question of group rights via the different but closely related concepts of human rights, the principle of non-discrimination, the principle of self-determination, and the concept of indigenous peoples. No doubt there are loose ends. The subject is inherently difficult and the literature, both legal and political, lacks coherence. Important links between categories are all too often ignored by single-issue enthusiasts and academic lobbyists. Moreover, the attempt at systematic treatment leads to generalization and an analytical structuring which is far too tidy. Room must be left for the distinguishing features of each society, and in New Zealand at least a major distinguishing feature is the significance accorded, both in law and in politics, to the Treaty of Waitangi.

The Treaty and its reinvigoration in recent times reminds us of the central problem. Most models of justice and human rights are based upon a historical status quo, and are not designed to change that status quo. If a radical adjustment of land distribution is to take place this is normally done by means of a legislative programme. In New Zealand the legislation based upon the Treaty of Waitangi has produced a pragmatic and somewhat half-hearted regime of transition.[21] Inevitably this regime must be based upon normal standards of non-discrimination. The consequence will be to produce tension between the idea of intercommunal equality and the more dynamic claims of historical equity and restitution derived from the Treaty and inhering in one community.

In my fourth and final lecture I shall try to bring the various strands together and to produce an inventory of the legal and constitutional vehicles which can be marshalled to cope with the agenda presented by the Treaty.

[21] See Ch. 1, n. 6 and text.

4

Waitangi: More a Problem than a Solution?

It is now time to produce a final report. Final, only in the sense of the structure of these lectures. The problems addressed are difficult, and my conclusions can only be provisional. Indeed, in New Zealand there is debate about the very content of the agenda, and final answers can only be expected when there is agreement about the questions that should appear on it.

Once again it is necessary to go back to the Treaty. It is by any standards an instrument from which heavy-duty performance is expected. At one and the same time it is a part of the mana of Maori, the source of a political agenda, and a means of achieving particular ends. Moreover, it is in reality the ancestor and inspiration of a line of legal developments, including sections 71[1] and 73[2] of the Constitution Act 1852, the Treaty of Waitangi Act 1975, and the Treaty of Waitangi (State Enterprises) Act 1988. The importance of the Treaty cannot be doubted, but the source of its importance bears further examination.

From the very early days its political and legal significance has been the subject of debate. Some Maori opinion regarded the Treaty as subversive of Maori

[1] See Ch. 2, n. 16.

[2] Section 73 secured the Crown's right of pre-emption acquired under Art. 2 of the Treaty. See Ch. 1, nn. 5 and 7. Notwithstanding the protective intention behind the provision, some gross abuses of the right occurred, as the Waitangi Tribunal's *Ngai Tahu Report* shows. See further Ch. 1, n. 5.

interest from the start, and some chiefs refused to sign it.[3] More recent Maori opinion appears to be varied, but the consensus is that the Treaty is an essential part of Maori heritage. At the same time, Mr Winston Peters MP[4] considers that there is too much focus on the Treaty, and that it has little to do with current Maori problems such as unemployment.

My view is that the Treaty provides a vehicle for legal developments, but that it is only a part of an assemblage of vehicles relevant to intercommunal relations. As a matter of common sense such a short text is obviously an imperfect means of resolving the complex issues presently on the agenda. This basic fact would remain even if all the textual problems concerning the Maori and English texts were to be settled. In any event the Treaty has several elements which, according to current conceptions of law and constitutional principle, are either eccentric or positively objectionable. In no special order the following eccentricities may be noted.

First, one of the purposes of the Treaty was to allow the immigration, specifically of 'British Subjects', from other British territories to the newly established colony. This purpose and its geopolitical background have both become defunct. Secondly, there was no representative democracy in New Zealand at the time the Treaty was concluded, but a traditional system of Chiefly authority. Nor did the Treaty envisage the introduction of democratic principles of government. This is not a criticism, of course, but it is necessary to recall the political context. Thirdly, the principle of pre-

[3] See Ch. 2, nn. 3 and 4, and text.

[4] See e.g. *New Zealand Parliamentary Debates*, 504 (1989), 14528–32, where Mr Peters emphasizes Maori rights to common citizenship under Art. 3 of the Treaty (and thus to equal opportunity with Pakeha in education and employment) rather than to 'partnership' or division of resources under Art. 2. (Mr Peters became Minister of Maori Affairs in the National Party (Conservative) Ministry which took office after the Labour defeat in the 1990 General Elections.)

emption,[5] even if well intentioned, was anomalous and discriminatory. It was abolished in 1865 when the Native Lands Act effectively nullified one aspect of Article 2 of the Treaty. No one has a present interest in restoring the right of pre-emption. Fourthly, there is the question of discovering the content of Article 2 in which the Queen undertook to protect the chiefs in the unqualified exercise of their chieftainship (te tino rangatiratanga) over their lands. This particular version of the text in English is supported by expert opinion.[6] Taking this version at face value, therefore, it is safe to make certain assumptions about what it does *not* mean. One such assumption is that it does not mean that tribal land, when it exists in appropriate form, can be subjected to chiefly and traditional forms of government to the exclusion of the normal system of representative democracy prevailing in New Zealand.

This assumption rests on two principles. First, such a result would be difficult to reconcile with the provisions of Article 3 of the Treaty, which establish the clear principle of common citizenship. Secondly, in case of doubt, the contemporary principles of human rights are supervenient and such principles lean towards equality and representative government. Indeed, if there were to be an insistence on the complete reinstatement of chiefly authority the exercise of such authority would, it can be presumed, involve substantial restrictions on the conditions under which individuals or groups of Maori could produce evidence of the necessary legal interest to bring a claim. The legislation of 1975 does not require claims to have chiefly sanction.

Those elements in the Treaty which are anachronistic and subject to desuetude should not be exaggerated.

[5] See Ch. 1, n. 5, and this Ch., n. 2.

[6] See the translation of Sir Hugh Kawharu (ed.), in *Waitangi: Māori and Pākehā Perspectives of the Treaty of Waitangi* (Auckland, 1989), quoted in Ch. 1 at n. 8. For a criticism of this view, see Sir Robin Cooke, Introduction to (1990) 14 *NZULR* (special Waitangi number) 1 at 3. And see Ch. 1, n. 5.

Such elements can be severed or ignored and it is perfectly normal for instruments long in force to be given creative and remedial interpretation. The Treaty cannot be set aside (even if that were constitutionally possible). Those who regard it as an exercise in hypocrisy or as the legal outwork of oppression—the normative panoply of colonial power—miss the point. Indeed, they miss the whole point of law. The words of a statute or a treaty have a life of their own and, except in certain extreme cases, the positive elements can be developed. After all is said and done, the hypocrisy of power gives hostages to fortune. For the determinist all is lost from the start, and the concept of law is essentially denied. What we should do, says the determinist—who often does not like lawyers as such—is to go home and wait for the revolution.

What we do have is the Treaty of Waitangi. It was not drafted by the Colonial Office but by Captain Hobson, assisted by others, on the basis of the muddled but, for their time, liberal prescriptions in the Instructions from Lord Normanby. The result was not all bad, and Dr Orange has pointed out that the Colonial Office was critical of the terms of the Treaty as concluded by Captain Hobson.[7] For if the Treaty were a simple expression of oppression it would not have been the source of embarrassment which it has been in practice.

What then are the vehicles and procedures available for the effective implementation of the principles of the Treaty of Waitangi? In spite of the problems noted, the first vehicle must still be the Treaty itself. Of course, its formal status is problematical, and it has not been *as such* the subject of general legislative incorporation. Moreover, it is not included in the draft Bill of Rights Bill[8] reported recently to the House of Representatives

[7] See C. Orange, *The Treaty of Waitangi* (Wellington, 1987), 98–100.

[8] Enacted as the New Zealand Bill of Rights Act 1990. See n. 29 below, and text.

by the Justice and Law Reform Committee: although the Bill (section 27) does save existing rights and freedoms. At the same time the Treaty has been given a high profile by the Crown, not least in the Treaty of Waitangi Act. Even if this were to be repealed, there is a calendar of claims[9] outstanding against the Crown based upon the Treaty. The Act thus constitutes a recognition of the legal validity of the Treaty, and its repeal would not impair that validity but would merely suspend the procedure for handling claims based upon the Treaty. Moreover, the legislative draftsman has used the phrase, 'the principles of the Treaty of Waitangi' and the judiciary is able to give appropriate substance to the phrase.[10]

Without canvassing all the evidence, there is room for the view that the Crown is at this stage estopped from denying the internal validity of the Treaty. There is also a certain indication that the Courts will refer to the Treaty to resolve difficulties in the application of legislation, even in the absence of express reference: compare Mr Justice Chilwell's judgment in the *Huakina* case (1987).[11] However, this type of recognition leaves the question of claims untouched, in the same way as a general clause in a Bill of Rights would not be self-executing. The internal implementation of the Treaty will involve a considerable apparatus, most of which cannot be said to be in place. The process of amendment of the Treaty of Waitangi Act suggests a lack of firm direction in so far as policy is reflected in legislation.

[9] See P. B. Temm, *The Waitangi Tribunal: The Conscience of the Nation* (Auckland, 1990), 14–16. Some 200 claims are outstanding. The increase in membership of the Tribunal under the Treaty of Waitangi Amendment Act 1988 is intended to help to deal with the backlog.

[10] See Ch. 1, nn. 25, 48–52 and text.

[11] *Huakina Development Trust* v. *Waikato Valley Authority* [1987] 2 NZLR 188, esp. at 206, 210. But see the reservations (*obiter*) of Casey and Hardie Boys JJ. in *Attorney-General* v. *New Zealand Maori Council* (No. 2) [1991] 2 NZLR 147 at 149.

At any rate, the Treaty remains central, although its status is a little mysterious. It is not an international agreement presently in force, since it could not survive the disappearance of one party as a result of its execution. Even if it were a valid international agreement, it would be subject to certain modifications, on the basis that particular obligations had been terminated as a result either of a fundamental change of circumstances or as a consequence of the emergence of new peremptory norms of general international law. For example, the right of pre-emption would, if it had survived, fall foul of the principle of non-discrimination on grounds of race, which forms a part of general international law and which falls within the class of peremptory norms.[12] In this same general context, if the Treaty were a valid international agreement, there might be some difficult questions of compatibility as between Waitangi and subsequent treaty obligations of the Crown in the sphere of human rights. In fact there are certain problems of compatibility with international standards, but they take a different form, as will be shown in due course.

Before other major vehicles of legal development and dispute settlement are considered, there are two topics which can be more or less set aside. The first is common-law aboriginal title to land. Whilst there is not scope here to do justice to this important subject, there are certain points which need to be made. First of all, there is no reason to regard aboriginal title as inimical to the application of the Treaty. It was in other times the failure of the Courts to apply the principle, rather than the principle itself, which called for criticism.[13]

[12] I. Brownlie, *Principles of Public International Law*, 4th edn. (Oxford, 1990), 512–13, 598–600.

[13] See the views of contributors to Kawharu (ed.), *Waitangi*, 10–12 (Brookfield), 50–3 (McHugh), and 92–117 (F. Hackshaw). Cf. Ch. 1, n. 23 and text above.

Secondly, the principle of common-law aboriginal title appears to be complementary to the operation of the Treaty, and compatible with public international law. After a cession the presumption is that private rights continue undisturbed, although the new sovereign has a liberty to make changes.[14] In fact in the Treaty of Waitangi the Crown promised not to exercise that liberty in respect of Maori land and other interests.

The second topic which needs to be recognized, but will not be pursued, is that of treaties made by the Crown in other regions, and especially in Canada. These treaties present similar problems, but they do not provide precise parallels with the Treaty of Waitangi, which was literally without precedent and which is unique in substance. At the same time, the Court of Appeal has derived assistance from the Canadian and United States experience of dealing with economic claims on a step-by-step basis.[15]

The vehicle which deserves substantial attention is undoubtedly the Waitangi Tribunal. The parent legislation of 1975 has the long title: 'An Act to provide for the observance, and confirmation, of the principles of the Treaty of Waitangi by establishing a Tribunal to make recommendations on claims relating to the practical application of the Treaty and to determine whether certain matters are consistent with the Treaty.' The basis of claim is very wide indeed. The requirements are twofold: the existence of legislation, or acts done by or on behalf of the Crown, which cause the claimant to be 'prejudicially affected'; and inconsistency of the legislation or act complained of with the principles[16] of the Treaty.

[14] See D. P. O'Connell, *State Succession in Municipal Law and International Law* (Cambridge, 1967), i. 107, 266; Brownlie, *Principles*, 4th edn., 657 (further references).

[15] See Sir Robin Cooke, Introduction to (1990) 14 *NZULR* 1 at 5.

[16] See Ch. 1, nn. 25, 48–52 and text.

The claimants must be Maori or of Maori descent. Claims must be brought by individuals but an individual may claim on behalf of a group. Whilst the Tribunal can only make recommendations, the Courts have been prepared to apply statutes in such a way as to give additional legal force to the work of the Tribunal. In any case, since 1988 in relation to State enterprises the Tribunal has the power to make binding decisions in certain cases.[17] Under legislation of 1985[18] the Tribunal has jurisdiction in respect of claims relating to prejudicial events which took place on or after 6 February 1840. The original legislation provides that the Tribunal can recommend either compensation or specific restitution if a claim is upheld.

By any standards the Waitangi Tribunal and its work so far constitute a remarkable phenomenon, and the Tribunal is the primary means of implementation of the promises of the Crown in the Treaty of 1840. None the less, the very existence of the Tribunal as a special or asymmetrical jurisdiction presents a good number of unresolved tensions and anomalies, the most obvious being the ambiguous approach to the legitimacy of the Treaty. It is not yet entrenched in a Bill of Rights, but is the basis for a special tribunal which in general has powers of recommendation only. No doubt there are political explanations for the form of the Act of 1975, but the somewhat half-hearted implementation of Waitangi creates an awkward gap between expectations and performance.

A second problem arises from the relation, in the sphere of land claims, between ordinary questions of title in which the basis of entitlement is the existence of an act contrary to the Treaty of Waitangi and claims under the Act of 1975. The answer to this is apparently obvious. The Act only permits claims against the

[17] See the Treaty of Waitangi (State Enterprises) Act 1988, section 10.
[18] Treaty of Waitangi Amendment Act 1985.

Crown. Claims against private individuals are excluded, and would inevitably collide with the Torrens system of registered title.[19] In any event, if revision of private titles was allowed with retroactive effect to 1840, the results would involve, or at least risk, infringements of human rights standards contained in international conventions by which New Zealand is bound.

But the restriction to claims against the Crown still presents anomalies. Even if breaches of the Treaty have resulted in the disposition of land in favour of private holders, and even if such transfers may not be reviewed, this does not rule out compensation by the Crown as a mode of redress. Moreover, the Act of 1975 relates to claims against the Crown and ignores the grey area consisting of episodes in the past in which the Crown failed to take effective action to prevent pressured sales or unofficial seizures.

There is another aspect of the work of the Tribunal which calls up doubts. The procedure is non-contentious, and this is deliberate. Moreover, the methods of taking evidence are flexible, and nowhere is it stated what the standard of proof of title should be. The result creates some unease in the observer. Certain of the claims, such as the *Ngai Tahu Claim*,[20] are very extensive, and have a public law dimension. In such cases the tasks imposed upoon the Tribunal are extremely onerous. Title is normally settled on a 'better title as between the two claimants' basis. However, in the land claims

[19] Established (now) by the Land Transfer Act 1952 (see G. W. Hinde, D. W. McMorland, and P. B. A. Sim, *Land Law*, i (1978), ch. 2). The possibility that Maori, common-law, 'non-territorial' rights or servitudes (see *Te Weehi* v. *Regional Fisheries Officer*, Ch. 1, n. 23) may survive over private land despite the general indefeasibility of registered titles, is suggested by P. G. McHugh in 'Aboriginal Servitudes and the Land Transfer Act' (1986) 16 *VUWLR* 313. *Sed quaere*; and see F. M. Brookfield, 'Maori Fishing Rights and the Fisheries Act 1983 . . .' [1987] *NZRL* 63 at 67.

[20] See now the Waitangi Tribunal's *Ngai Tahu Report* (Wai-27, 1991), in which the Tribunal has made seriously adverse findings against the Crown in respect of its acquisition by pre-emption of most of the South Island. See Ch. 1, n. 5 and this Ch., n. 2.

involving tribal entitlements and cross-claims it is desirable that a multilaterally valid title emerge if existing titles are to be disturbed.

In any event, the Tribunal's jurisdiction is confined to disputes between Maori and the Crown and disputes between Maori are excluded. However, the evidence of competing claimants must be relevant to the validity of claims against the Crown, and it would be invidious if such claims could only come in for the purpose of tripping up claims against the Crown.

There are other sources of difficulty. The relation between the Tribunal and the hierarchy of Maori Land Courts appears to be unclear. Moreover the *locus standi* for claims is based on the private law concept and tribes as such have no legal standing, which is ironical, given the tribal role in the conclusion of the original Treaty. Certainly the issue of cross-claims requires statutory solution.[21]

The piecemeal approach of the 1975 Act and the important ramifications of individual land claims, both for other relevant entitlements and for land-use planning and development, lead to thoughts of practical improvement. The indecisiveness of the mechanism for making claims is disturbing. No doubt the Tribunal can and does mount its own research operations, but this is not the equivalent of bringing other claims into account in a procedural sense. The result is rather wasteful, since all that can be done is to evaluate the particular claim, and a great deal of work may result in an indecisive finding. It is clear that some important claims relate to land and resources, or resources alone, as in the case of fisheries, and that such claims often have environmental implications. Indeed, the Parliamentary Commissioner for the Environment has been directly involved in the follow-up to the findings of the Tribunal.[22]

[21] See Ch. 1, n. 47 and text.

[22] See Ch. 1, n. 27 and text.

It would surely be an improvement if the Tribunal had access to a Commission which could provide a land use and planning assessment of the larger land and resource claims. The benefits of such assessment would be enormous, and would involve taking account of the general public interest. The difficulty, of course, is that such planning assessment would be relatively pointless unless the findings of the Tribunal on title are more decisive and more multilateral than they presently are.

In general, the ramifications of findings of the Waitangi Tribunal need more attention, not only in the interests of Maori claimants but in the overall interest of the *two* communities in stability of dealing and optimum utilization of resources.

The ordinary Courts, and especially the Court of Appeal, have an important auxiliary role in the recognition of the principles of Waitangi and their practical application. In particular, as in the *Maori Council* case,[23] the Courts have had to play a forward role in maintaining some kind of coherence in the system and in seeking a balancing of interests. In mounting such necessary rescue operations, the Courts appear to have ventured near the normal bounds of justiciability.[24] This is an observation and not a criticism. It is arid to criticize the Courts for intervention, and judges are too often damned if they do and damned if they don't.

Of course, the Courts can only carry out judicial review if an applicant takes the initiative. The famous decision of the Court of Appeal on the State Owned Enterprises Act resulted from an application brought by the New Zealand Maori Council.[25] In the words of Mr Justice Casey in the Court of Appeal in 1987: 'The

[23] [1987] 1 NZLR 641.

[24] Cf. the more extremely expressed view of J. Kelsey, *A Question of Honour? Labour and the Treaty, 1984—1989* (Wellington, 1990), 237, that the Courts 'even deviated from their designated constitutional role and actively facilitated political resolution of treaty disputes'.

[25] Established under the Maori Community Development Act 1962.

New Zealand Maori Council . . . has among its functions the conservation and advancement of virtually every aspect of Maori life. It claims to represent and speak for a large proportion of Maori people and its standing (along with that of its Chairman in his own right) to bring these proceedings could not be challenged.'[26]

The Waitangi Tribunal, the ordinary Courts, and various bodies such as the Maori Council and Maori Trust Boards,[27] constitute the principal sources of decision-making and public initiative. Apart from these, there are normative sources of change and development, the most obvious of which would be the entrenchment of the Treaty of Waitangi in a Bill of Rights. The proposed Bill of Rights of 1985, which was to have been entrenched, gave a prominent place to the Treaty whilst also emphasizing international standards of human rights.[28] Its long title and preamble read:

An Act to institute as the supreme law of New Zealand a Bill of Rights in order to affirm, protect and promote human rights and fundamental freedoms in New Zealand, and to recognize and affirm the Treaty of Waitangi.

WHEREAS

(1) New Zealand is a democratic society based on the rule of law and on principles of freedom, equality and the dignity and worth of the human person;
(2) New Zealand in 1978 ratified the International Covenant on Civil and Political Rights;
(3) The Maori people, as tangata whenua o Aotearoa, and the Crown entered in 1840 into a solemn compact, known as Te Tiriti o Waitangi or the Treaty of

[26] [1987] 1 NZLR 641 at 697.

[27] See the Maori Trust Boards Act 1955.

[28] See 'A Bill of Rights for New Zealand' (Government White Paper, 1985) and the *Final Report* thereon by the Justice and Law Reform Committee (1988), and see next n.

Waitangi, and it is desirable to recognize and affirm the Treaty as part of the supreme law of New Zealand;

(4) It is desirable to affirm the human rights and fundamental freedoms of all the people of New Zealand without discrimination and to ensure their recognition and observance as part of the supreme law of New Zealand by the Parliament and Government of New Zealand.

Part 2 of the Bill was entitled 'The Treaty of Waitangi' and consisted of a single article as follows:

4. The Treaty of Waitangi
   (1) The rights of the Maori people under the Treaty of Waitangi are hereby recognized and affirmed.
   (2) The Treaty of Waitangi shall be regarded as always speaking and shall be applied to circumstances as they arise so that effect may be given to its spirit and true intent.
   (3) The Treaty of Waitangi means the Treaty as set out in English and Maori in the Schedule to this Bill of Rights.

In addition Article 26 provided as follows:

Where in any proceeding before any court, any question arises whether any enactment or rule of law, or any act or policy, is consistent with the Treaty of Waitangi, the court may on the application of any party to the proceeding or of its own motion refer that question to the Waitangi Tribunal for a report and opinion, and the court shall have regard to that report and opinion.

This proposal was not proceeded with and there had been considerable political opposition from Maori to the idea of entrenchment.

The more recent Bill of Rights[29] (as reported from the Justice and Law Reform Committee of the House of Representatives on 17 July 1990) contains no reference to the Treaty of Waitangi, although there is a savings

[29] Enacted, without attempt at entrenchment, as the New Zealand Bill of Rights Act 1990. See Ch. 1, n. 21, Ch. 2, n. 6, and text. Sections 27 and 19 referred to became ss. 28 and 20 in the Bill as enacted.

clause for other rights and freedoms in Article 27. The approach is based on the incorporation of New Zealand's obligations arising from its adherence to the International Covenant on Civil and Political Rights and its title is as follows:

An Act—

(*a*) To affirm, protect, and promote human rights and fundamental freedoms in New Zealand; and
(*b*) To affirm New Zealand's commitment to the International Covenant on Civil and Political Rights.

Article 19 of the new Bill is headed 'Rights of Minorities' and provides as follows:

Rights of minorities—A person who belongs to an ethnic, religious, or linguistic minority in New Zealand shall not be denied the right, in community with other members of that minority, to enjoy the culture, to profess and practice the religion, or to use the language, of that minority.

This provision is derived from Article 27 of the Covenant, which uses the rather old-fashioned term 'minorities' but is in essence unobjectionable.

Does it really matter whether a Bill of rights expressly includes the principles of the Treaty of Waitangi? Leaving aside questions of political tactics concerning the possibility of amendments to the Bill of Rights, the answer is both yes and no. On the one hand, as a question of prestige and constitutional status, reference to the Treaty in a Bill of Rights is of great importance. That is a question of political symbolism. On the other hand, the principles of the Treaty, if incorporated into the law in that form, would coexist with the principles of human rights law which would also be affirmed in any contemporary Bill of Rights. This coexistence would be even more significant if the incorporation of human rights standards took the form of express reference to the International Covenant on Civil and

Political Rights. In this context, the principles of the Treaty of Waitangi must be applied on the basis of compatibility with the international obligations of New Zealand concerning human rights and fundamental freedoms. This question of compatibility is probably at least as important as the issue of incorporation of Waitangi in a Bill of Rights and will persist whether or not such incorporation takes place.

Consideration must now be given to the all-important question of the treaty obligations of New Zealand in respect of human rights. There can be no question that these obligations are of significance for the resolution of questions of group rights and relations between the communities. As already noted, New Zealand has become a party to virtually all the multilateral standard-setting conventions concerning human rights. The relevant conventions include the following:

The International Covenant on Economic, Social and Cultural Rights.[30]

The International Covenant on Civil and Political Rights.[31]

The International Convention on the Elimination of All Forms of Racial Discrimination.[32]

The Convention on the Elimination of All Forms of Discrimination against Women.[33]

The Convention on the Political Rights of Women.[34]

The Convention on the Prevention and Punishment of the Crime of Genocide.[35]

The UNESCO Convention against Discrimination in Education.[36]

[30] See Ch. 1, n. 56. [31] Ibid.

[32] *Multilateral Treaties in Respect of which the Secretary-General Performs Depositary Functions: List of Signatures, Ratifications, Accessions, etc., as at 31 December 1989*, 106; I. Brownlie, *Basic Documents on Human Rights*, 2nd edn. (Oxford, 1981), 150.

[33] *Multilateral Treaties*, 170; Brownlie, *Basic Documents*, 94.

[34] *Multilateral Treaties*, 615; Brownlie, *Basic Documents*, 91.

[35] *Multilateral Treaties*, 97; Brownlie, *Basic Documents*, 31.

[36] *UNTS*, 429, p. 93; Brownlie, *Basic Documents*, 234.

These conventions face the usual problem of implementation within the legal system of New Zealand. Treaties may bind the Crown externally, on the plane of international law, but normally they are enforceable as part of municipal law only if they are expressly incorporated by legislation.[37] In the absence of such incorporation, the conventions provide aids to the interpretation of statutes, because the principle is that a statute is presumed to be compatible with the international obligations of the Crown.[38] This is particularly the case when the statute concerned recites that its purpose is to implement a Convention even if actual incorporation is avoided. Moreover, there is reason to believe that reference to the treaty obligations of the Crown would be relevant to the review of the exercise of a discretion conferred by legislation: see the analogy of *Van Gorkom* v. *A.-G.* (affirmed on other grounds in the Court of Appeal), decided by Cooke J.[39]

Legislative recognition of the Treaty of Waitangi will inevitably ride alongside legislative implementation of the treaty obligations in human rights matters. In this context it is of great interest to note that New Zealand has ratified the Optional Protocol to the International Covenant on Civil and Political Rights[40] and thus accepted the competence of the Human Rights Committee which monitors compliance with the Covenant. In particular, the Committee has the competence 'to receive and consider communications from individuals subject to its jurisdiction who claim to be victims of a

[37] See *Ashby* v. *Attorney-General*, High Court of New Zealand (1981, unreported); Judgment of the Chief Justice quoted by J. B. Elkind and A. Shaw, 55 *BYIL* (1984), 225–6. See the same case on appeal *sub nom. Ashby* v. *Minister of Immigration* [1981] 1 NZLR 222 at 224 (Cooke J.), 229 (Richardson J.); cf. Somers J. at 232.

[38] See e.g. *Post Office* v. *Estuary Radio* [1967] 1 WLR 1396, CA, at 1404 (Diplock LJ delivering the judgment of the Court).

[39] [1977] 1 NZLR 535. And see *Ashby* v. *Minister of Immigration* [1981] 1 NZLR 222 at 226 (Cooke J.), 229 (Richardson J.), 232 (Somers J.).

[40] See Ch. 1, n. 57.

violation' by the State concerned of any of the rights set forth in the Covenant. Complainants must have exhausted all available domestic remedies. Subject to that condition, complaints may take the form of a written communication. The functions of the Committee do not involve a public and judicial determination of issues. However, the 'views' of the Committee on individual communications, which are submitted to the Governments concerned, in substance involve decisions of law and fact, and the Respondent State has a duty to produce explanations and to report the remedial steps which may have been taken.

In any event the human rights standards contained in the conventions to which New Zealand is a party, together with the principles of general international law which form part of municipal law without express incorporation and unless excluded by the express words of a statute,[41] provide an extensive source of techniques for balancing interests and, if necessary, supporting affirmative action. Moreover, the relevant multilateral treaties provide authority for resort to affirmative action, whilst also placing certain constraints upon such policies. Article 2, para. 2, of the International Convention on the Elimination of All Forms of Racial Discrimination of 1966 provides that:[42]

> States Parties shall, when the circumstances so warrant, take, in the social, economic, cultural and other fields, special and concrete measures to ensure the adequate development and protection of certain racial groups or individuals belonging to them, for the purpose of guaranteeing them the full and equal enjoyment of human rights and fundamental freedoms. These measures shall in no case entail as a consequence the maintenance of unequal or separate rights for different racial groups after the objectives for which they were taken have been achieved.

[41] Brownlie, *Principles*, 43–7.

[42] See n. 32 above.

A similar approach is to be found in Article 4, para. 1, of the Convention on the Elimination of All Forms of Discrimination against Women, 1980, which provides that:[43]

> Adoption by States Parties of temporary special measures aimed at accelerating *de facto* equality between men and women shall not be considered discrimination as defined in the present Convention, but shall in no way entail as a consequence the maintenance of unequal or separate standards; these measures shall be discontinued when the objectives of equality of opportunity and treatment have been achieved.

The presence of these elements of flexibility and controlled affirmative action strongly suggests that the stock of human rights conventions, together with principles derived from general international law, provide very adequate means for the management of intercommunal relations and associated issues. It is for this and other reasons that there are no substantial attractions in invoking the legal concept of indigenous peoples in the New Zealand context. The pattern of means for the recognition and protection of group rights is rich and far from inadequate. The concept of indigenous peoples would introduce a disharmony since it does not claim equality but a qualitatively separate status. It places ethnic and communal values above all else and in principle involves a priority over human rights values.

In my opinion the concept of indigenous peoples and the protective segregation it involves in practice is only appropriate when the special vulnerability of the group calls for special measures amounting to a rescue operation. Whether that is so is, of course, a question of fact. In any event the situation in this country is

[43] *Multilateral Treaties*, 170; Brownlie, *Basic Documents*, 94. New Zealand ratified the Convention on 10 Jan. 1985.

governed by the principles of the Treaty of Waitangi and the regime is *sui generis*. The protection of group rights results from a combination of human rights standards and the principles of the Treaty of Waitangi.

The account of the series of agencies and sources of legal development relevant to the resolution of inter-communal questions being now complete, it remains to focus upon certain issues presented by the Treaty of Waitangi and the expectations usually built upon it. There is no doubt that land rights should head the list in practice. In reality this item splits into several distinct questions.

The first is the detection and remedying of unjust confiscations[44] and cases of land transferred on conditions which were subsequently disregarded,[45] in each case involving acts of the Crown and land of which the Crown now has the power of disposition. The second concerns unjust transfers involving private interests and land not presently vested in the Crown. The third is the implied undertaking contained in the second article of the Treaty of Waitangi and confirmed by Lord Normanby's Instructions,[46] that is, the understanding that the Maori would be left with a reasonable proportion of land for their own use. The fourth question is the extent to which the rights guaranteed by the Treaty extend to natural resources other than land, such as fisheries or coal reserves.

The first question—the unjust confiscations and claims in respect of land received by the Crown—is addressed by the legislation creating the Waitangi Tribunal, though the system has drawbacks. The fourth question has also been addressed without too much difficulty. The provisions of Article 2 of the Waitangi Treaty apply to fisheries and the problem outstanding

[44] See Ch. 1, n. 7.
[45] See the *Ngai Tahu Report*, Ch. 1, n. 5, and this Ch., n. 20.
[46] Quoted in text at Ch. 2, n. 5.

is not the entitlement but the absence of a statutory mechanism for the effective vindication of rights of fishery. Moreover, in the *Tainui* decision[47] the Court of Appeal showed a strong tendency to recognize the substance of things and to treat rights to mine coal as interests in land for statutory purposes, and to do this in the course of protecting the Maori interest in claims pending before the Waitangi Tribunal.

The second and third questions—forced transfers not involving the Crown and the issue of the proportion of lands involved in sales—are not addressed by recent developments. To this might be added the fact that no provision is made for claims on behalf of tribes or between tribes. Here as elsewhere there can be detected an unstable borderland between public and private law concepts and remedies.

Competing with the question of land rights there is the issue of sovereignty and the concept of te tino rangatiratanga in the second article of the Treaty, which Sir Hugh Kawharu translates as 'the unqualified exercise of their chieftainship'.[48] It is not my intention to propose a solution to the problem of interpretation. It will be assumed, however, for the sake of argument, that the Maori text governs, and that the correct meaning of the Maori text is that there was to be power sharing, and that the traditional Maori structure of authority was to be maintained. The literature tends to avoid facing up to the implications of this view. Moreover, there is a certain tendency to confuse the question of authority and the business of preserving Maori customs and traditions more generally.

The issue which needs to be faced is that a strict adherence to chieftainship and values based upon birth and status would inevitably be incompatible with contemporary democratic values and standards of

[47] *Tainui Maori Trust Board* v. *Attorney-General* [1989] 2 NZLR 513.
[48] See Ch. 1, n. 15 and this Ch., n. 6.

human rights. In other words, on this view the problem is not ultimately one of translation but of the compatibility of the Treaty with other obligations and standards binding the Government of New Zealand. If care is not taken, the restitutionary aspects of Waitangi will appear to be flawed by an appeal to a value system incompatible with the idea of political democracy. It is probable that the Treaty has always rested on certain conceptions which are in tension with each other. The idea of rangatiratanga in the second Article is difficult to reconcile with the idea of common citizenship which is expressed in the third Article. At times in the nineteenth century it looked as if it would be possible to establish more or less autonomous areas in which Maori custom would be prevalent.[49] No such development took place, and the fact is that the concept of the individual alienation of land was, from the start, inimical to the preservation of the integrity of tribal domains and the attendant chiefly authority.

A more practical issue connected with the Treaty is the protection of the cultural values of the Maori. Article 2 of the Treaty can be said to protect such values but clearly does not provide any detailed guarantees. However, in the *Te Reo Maori* claim[50] the Waitangi Tribunal found that the Maori language is a taonga guaranteed protection under the terms of Article 2 of the Treaty and that the protection guaranteed requires active and not merely passive protection.[51] The Tribunal consequently held to the effect that:[52]

[49] Autonomous areas in fact existed, *de facto* in status in relation to the colonial legal order: see Ch. 2, n. 14; also Ch. 2, n. 16 and text.

[50] See *Finding of the Waitangi Tribunal relating to Te Reo Maori . . .* (Wai-11, 1986).

[51] Ibid. 28–9.

[52] For the consequential recommendations, see ibid. 71–2. For the ensuing litigation, in relation to Maori broadcasting, see *Attorney-General* v. *New Zealand Maori Council* [1991] 2 NZLR 129 and *Attorney-General* v. *New Zealand Maori Council* (No. 2) [1991] 2 NZLR 147, together with *Report of The Waitangi Tribunal on Claims concerning the Allocation of Radio Frequencies* (Wai 26 and Wai 150, 1990). See also A. L. Mikaere [1991] NZRL Rev. 149 at 151–5 and 157–8.

1. Law and policies preventing the use of Maori in the Courts are inconsistent with the principles of the Treaty.[53]
2. The education and broadcasting systems overemphasize English and thus fail to give adequate protection to the Maori language.
3. The Maori language should be recognized in the Courts and in dealing with any department or local authority.

The Tribunal also recommended the setting up of a Maori Language Commission. The recommendations have been partially implemented by the passing of the Maori Language Act 1987.[54]

Until the international obligations of the Crown are more fully implemented within the sphere of internal law, the reliance upon Article 2 of the Treaty of Waitangi will no doubt continue. Yet that Article states an entitlement without much more. The international conventions provide a much more helpful code of principles for dealing with the sophisticated issues of equality and non-discrimination in education and broadcasting.

The last issue is that of demographic change. Whilst it is true that the Treaty of Waitangi legitimated immigration of British subjects, the underlying assumption, reflected clearly in Lord Normanby's Instructions to Captain Hobson, was that adequate lands and resources would be available for the Maori. Consequently, the Maori community has a legitimate

[53] For the then legal position (as it stood before the Maori Language Act 1987, section 4, came into force on 1 Feb. 1988), see *Mihaka* v. *Police* [1980] 1 NZLR 453; and see next n.

[54] Principally the Act (as amended in 1991) set up Te Taura Whiri I Te Reo Maori (Maori Language Commission) (sections 6–14), declared Maori to be 'an official language' (section 3), and provided for the right to speak it in legal proceedings (section 4). No specific provision was made for the official use of Maori otherwise, either in regard to (*a*) court documents or (*b*) business with government departments or local authorities. As to (*a*) the position arguably may have been affected by the repeal in New Zealand of the early English legislation relied on by Bisson J. in *Mihaka* v. *Police* [1980] 1 NZLR 453 at 459, by the Imperial Laws Application Act 1988, section 4.

interest in the ethnic composition of New Zealand as a whole and in the population densities of the various regions.

The more detailed tasks of this study now completed, it is time to return to the broader questions of law and morality which lie behind the debate about Waitangi. In the first lecture these broader questions were formulated in terms of equity as between early and subsequent arrivals. As a matter of general international law, as reflected in multilateral conventions to which New Zealand is a party, the applicable standards do not depend on the priority of settlement. Human rights standards prescribe non-discrimination on the basis of race, national or social origin, property, birth, or other status. The principle is thus one of common citizenship and equality of status.

Within this framework of equality there is room for affirmative action to maintain cultural autonomy and the protection of languages and other indicia of group identity. At the same time, there are certain issues in relation to which special standards or criteria apply and these special standards derive from the Treaty of Waitangi, particularly with reference to recognition of land rights. However, it is possible that in this respect the Treaty complements and reinforces the principle of non-discrimination so that the promises of the Crown are seen as an unconscious anticipation of contemporary standards of racial equality.

This complementarity between human rights standards and the principles of Waitangi, however, fails to work in two areas of contention. First, it fails if the Treaty is used as a basis for the maintenance or rehabilitation of customs incompatible with human rights standards: in the real world this usually involves the issue of equality of women. Secondly, if the provisions of Articles 1 and/or 2 of the Treaty are interpreted so as to justify the reinstitution of the autonomous political authority of the tribes and their chiefs, this will also pose serious problems of compatibility with human rights standards bearing upon social equality and representative democracy.

The linguistic argument, that in 1840 the chiefs only ceded kawanatanga and that the chiefs regarded the result as a relation of protection and not annexation, is fully appreciated. The contention is whether the exponents of this view are willing to face up to the legal and political ramifications. It would be a strange result if the Treaty of Waitangi, which has many virtues and was in its time seen as exceptionally liberal, should become a vehicle for demands which are in social terms reactionary.

Glossary

iwi	tribe
hapu	sub-tribe
kawanatanga	governance, trusteeship
mana	authority, prestige, sovereignty
marae	village courtyard; the spiritual and symbolic centre for tribal affairs
Pakeha	European (not Maori)
rangatiratanga	chieftainship, authority
raupatu	the confiscation of land
taiapure	special part of the sea for Maori use
tangata whenua	person or people of a given place
taonga	treasures, cultural heritage
tino rangatiratanga, te	the unqualified exercise of (their) chieftainship, highest chieftainship
wahi tapu	sacred places

Index

The manufacturer's authorised representative in the EU for product safety is Oxford University Press España S.A. of el Parque Empresarial San Fernando de Henares, Avenida de Castilla, 2 – 28830 Madrid (www.oup.es/en or product.safety@oup.com). OUP España S.A. also acts as importer into Spain of products made by the manufacturer.

www.ingramcontent.com/pod-product-compliance
Lightning Source LLC
LaVergne TN
LVHW101441200926
848483LV00001B/7
9780198257165